# Dispute Resolution: Expert Determination

## John Kendall
*Solicitor*

LONGMAN

© Longman Group UK Ltd 1992

ISBN 0 85121 798 2

*Published by*
Longman Law, Tax and Finance
Longman Group UK Ltd
21–27 Lamb's Conduit Street, London WC1N 3NJ

*Associated offices*
Australia, Hong Kong, Malaysia, Singapore, USA

Printed in Great Britain by Biddles of Guildford Ltd

# Contents

x CONTENTS

# Preface

I had a traditional legal education in the early 1970s. The courses contained little or nothing about dispute resolution, and I had never heard of arbitration. As an articled clerk (as trainee solicitors were then called) one of my tasks was to proof read agreements. I then encountered, for the first time, the phrase 'as an expert and not as an arbitrator'.

Lawyers from a number of different disciplines encounter expert determination. Property specialists can refer to Bernstein and Reynolds' *Handbook of Rent Review*; statistically rent review is by far and away the most significant application; but other uses of expert determination are not covered in any book. Some of the arbitration textbooks touch on the principles of expert determination, but only as a side-issue to their central topic. Law libraries do not have a separate category for this subject, and it is usually treated as a subdivision of arbitration, from which it is rather different.

Further confusion is created by the use of the word 'expert', which makes most people think of an 'expert witness', which is hardly surprising given the great importance of expert witnesses in modern dispute resolution. The function of the expert to whom issues are referred is not, like the expert witness, to give evidence about those issues to a tribunal, but to determine those issues himself. The word 'expert' does have to be used for our topic because 'valuer', the only real alternative, no longer covers all the applications of the procedure, particularly those which have been developed more recently.

So, finding frequent enquiries being made to my firm about determination by experts in applications other than rent review, I decided to write this book. I hope it will be useful to practitioners from all sides of the civil law, both those who draft agreements providing for the use of expert determination and those litigators like myself who advise on the interpretation of expert clauses and on the conduct of the references themselves. For those readers who are not litigators I have included a glossary of terms connected with expert determination which derive mainly from the way the courts have approached the subject and from allied questions arising from litigation and arbitration.

I have drawn on the experience of specialists from every department of my firm. I am very grateful in particular to the following colleagues: Deborah Adams, Martin Bates, Paul Bedford, Kate Buckley, Doran Doeh, Ian Elder, Richard Everett, Ian Ferguson, Judith Gill, Jonathan Hitchin, Rupert Jones, Sarah Jones, Don McGown, William Norris, John Rink, Sara Robinson, Jeremy Sharman, Derek Sloan and Allan Tyrer. Malek Ali, Sally Brooks, Antony Fobel, Jason Hambury and Brian Rook, who were trainee solicitors at the time, and my secretary Carol Carder, all did very useful research and checking. Outside Allen & Overy I have to thank Stewart Boyd, Malcolm Clarke, Stephen Coleman, John Dick, Andrew Dobson, Brian Granger, Mark McGaw, Peter McMahon, Robert Morgan, Michael Renshall, Shaun Stewart, Christopher Thomas and John Uff. Lastly I must thank my wife Jenny for all her help in getting this book ready for publication.

Having had so much help, I am responsible for any errors that remain: and the expressions of opinion are my own.

I apologise for having found it easier to keep to the sexist tradition of referring to parties and experts as 'he', and the colonialist tradition of referring to Wales as 'England', and hope this will not offend readers. I have tried to state the law as at 31 October 1991.

*John Kendall*
*9 Cheapside*
*London EC2V 6AD*

# Table of Cases

# Table of Legislation

## Table of Statutes

## Table of Statutory Instruments

# Table of Conventions

# Abbreviations

Bernstein and Reynolds — their book on rent review: see further reading.

FIDIC — Federation Internationale des Ingenieurs-Conseils and the international engineering contract they publish under the same initials.

ICE — the Institute of Civil Engineers and the engineering contract they publish under the same initials.

ICAEW — the Institute of Chartered Accountants in England and Wales.

ICLR — the International Construction Law Review.

ISVA — the Incorporated Society of Valuers and Auctioneers.

Mustill and Boyd — their book on arbitration: see Further Reading.

RICS — the Royal Institution of Chartered Surveyors.

RSC — Rules of the Supreme Court.

# Chapter 1

# Introduction

## 1.1 General remarks

### 1.1.1 A simple procedure

Expert determination is a means by which the parties to a contract jointly instruct a third party to decide an issue. The third party is now commonly known as an expert, usually because he has been chosen for his expertise about the issue between the parties. The practice is found in a wide range of commercial applications, from rent reviews to breach of warranty claims, and from construction disputes to pension scheme transfers. The essential element in each case is the manner in which the expert decides the issue. The procedure is simple and based on the wording of each contract adopting expert determination: precedents used in the various applications do not vary greatly from each other. Expert determination had its origin in non-contentious valuation. It has increasingly been used for technical as well as valuation issues, and for dispute resolution. It is quick, cheap and private. It is used to resolve issues about both small and large sums: the amounts at stake sometimes run into tens of millions of pounds. The continuing adaptation and development of expert determination into new areas show that its usefulness is appreciated by both businessmen and lawyers.

### 1.1.2 Arbitration is different

The study of expert determination has traditionally been attached to the study of arbitration. While the procedures have many similarities, the differences have created a great deal of confusion, and it is for this reason that the whole of Chapter 15 is devoted to an explanation of the distinction between arbitration and expert determination. Experts are often loosely described as

1

being some kind of arbitrator. The fact is that they are not. Experts are a distinct species of dispute resolver whose activities are subject to little or no control by the court, from whose decisions there is no appeal, but who may nevertheless be liable for negligence in performing these otherwise unreviewable functions. Arbitrators, by contrast, are subject to control by the court, some of their decisions are, at least in theory, subject to appeal, and they are immune from actions for negligence. A partnership or company can be an expert, whereas an arbitral tribunal always consists of readily identifiable individuals.

### 1.1.3 Enforcement and international contracts

Another important difference from arbitration is in the area of enforcement. Experts' decisions have a completely different status from arbitration awards or judgments of the court. Outside of insolvency procedures, experts' decisions cannot be enforced without further court action wherever enforcement is sought. This means that expert determination is of little use in cases where international enforcement is required, as experts' decisions cannot be enforced like arbitration awards under the 1958 New York Convention or like judgments of courts of European Community countries under the 1968 Brussels Convention. Despite these drawbacks, and while this book describes only the English law and practice relating to expert determination, the procedure is found in other jurisdictions: there have been some important Australian judgments on disputed expert determinations, and there are cases on the subject in the New Zealand law reports. Outside the common law, the French practice of *mandataires* has similar characteristics, see para 216 ff of de Boisseson's textbook on French Arbitration law (listed in Further Reading): and there are comparable procedures in Germany, Italy and the Netherlands.

### 1.1.4 From valuer to expert and dispute resolver

The development of the procedure from its origins in valuation to modern 'expert' applications has led me to attempt to distinguish between these two types and to classify applications either as belonging to the traditional, valuation type, or as owing more to the concept of a technical expert, which I have labelled 'industrial'. This distinction becomes clearer when one sees that it is mainly the industrial applications which have developed into dispute resolution. The use of the label 'expert' is now well recognised. The clause in a contract which refers matters to an expert for determination is known in this book as the 'expert clause'.

### 1.1.5 Statutory valuers excluded

Some valuers, such as district valuers, operate by statute, and numerous dispute resolvers, such as the Insurance Ombudsman, have recently been established by statute. This book does not deal with any of them, and is limited to the study of valuers and experts appointed under the terms of contracts. This contract-based private law does not apply to officials operating under a statute: see 14.9.2.

### 1.1.6 ADR experts excluded

Experts are also used in some forms of Alternative Dispute Resolution, or ADR. This book does not deal with that use of experts, but does show (in Chapter 16) how expert determination can be used as a form of ADR, with the added advantage of producing a binding result: most forms of ADR produce a non-binding result.

## 1.2 Sources of law and information

### 1.2.1 Origins and options

There is nothing very new about expert determination. It has been a feature of English commercial and legal practice for at least 250 years. The first reported case is found in 1754: *Belchier v Reynolds* 3 Keny 88. The procedure originated to deal with circumstances where parties wish to set up machinery for determining a price without negotiations, often where the obligation to make a payment arises in the future, as with options. An option is, typically, a contract, a deed or a provision made by a testator in his will by which one party grants to the other the right to buy property, from him or his estate, at a future date. An option may say that the price for the purchase at that future date will be determined by a valuer acting as an expert if the parties cannot agree on the price at that time.

### 1.2.2. Contract law

Expert determination is found in contracts between two parties; the only occasions when more than two parties are involved are found in the valuation of shares in companies, but there again the parties are bound together by arrangements analogous to contracts. When there are disputes about expert determination, the courts apply the law of contract, and the law of contract is the most important area of law for this subject. Thus, while all the usual contractual rules about offer and acceptance, consideration, intention to create legal relations, illegality, mistake, misrepresentation, repudiation, breach, discharge and so forth are relevant to understanding the contractual context of the reference to the expert, those rules may also have a direct bearing on whether a decision of an expert can be enforced.

### 1.2.3 The law reports

The most significant source of the law about expert determination is the law reports. This book does not cite all the cases on the subject, and does not cite a case where to do so would serve only to record the existence of that case, with no other purpose. The law reports also provide information about the applications of the procedure. But the law reports are a random collection of cases, and the very fact that each of those cases resulted from a dispute which the parties could not settle by agreement and had to take to court may make them an unrepresentative sample of the applications of the procedure. Another random factor is the accident of reporting: as can be seen from the list of cases, there were four important unreported English cases between 1987 and 1990. The most important recent decision, *Jones v Sherwood Computer Services plc* [1991] NPC 60, was first published outside LEXIS eighteen months after the judgment following a complaint from the judge in *Nikko Hotels (UK) Ltd v MEPC plc* [1991] 28 EG 86 that it had not been reported. The NPC (New Property Cases) series of reports are read by property specialists. *Jones v Sherwood* was about the sale of a business and should have been reported in one of the principal general series.

### 1.2.4 Practice

Although not a true source in that it is not found in published material, the other main source of information about the applications of expert determination is provided by the instances encountered in the course of practice. Practice is, of course, even less representative than the law reports, but it does have the advantage of providing examples of the use of expert determination where there were no recorded disputes.

*1.2.5. Statutes*

No statute deals with the subject and the citation of statutes in this book is necessary mainly because of the need to draw a distinction between expert determination and arbitration.

*1.2.6 Confidentiality*

The privacy of expert determination significantly reduces the volume of available information. References to experts are private in the same way that arbitrations are. While this is an advantage for the parties, it does not facilitate studying the subject. First, there is no system at all for publishing information about individual determinations, or about the subject generally: and secondly, the parties themselves often agree to keep details of their cases confidential, and that agreement is a binding contractual obligation. So the capacity to make a thorough survey of the subject is inhibited by one of its most important characteristics.

## 1.3 Method

*1.3.1 Evolution through commercial practice*

The study of expert determination is not just the study of a procedure for settling issues. The subject is defined by its applications. All the applications of expert determination have evolved through commercial practice. Hence Chapters 2–7 look at the applications in detail.

*1.3.2 Difference from studying litigation and arbitration*

In this respect the study of expert determination is rather unusual. The study of litigation or arbitration does not depend on detailed study of the applications of those systems. Both arbitration and litigation have an independent existence beyond any specific application, because they can be used very widely for all kinds of dispute resolution. Expert determination has, until recently, been limited to the applications set out in Chapters 2–7. However, the trend is growing for expert determination to be used to resolve all aspects of a dispute arising under a contract, and not just one category of technical aspects. If this trend continues, the details of the applications may cease to matter. But that stage is still some way off. In the meantime, therefore, the applications are an integral part of a study of expert determination.

### 1.3.3 Focus on traditional form

This book concentrates on expert determination where the expert is appointed by the parties to a contract to make a decision which is final and binding on them. To maintain this focus, the book does not dwell much on forms of expert determination where the decision is not made by a third party or the decision is interim. For the former, see 6.3.5, and for the construction contract examples of the latter, 6.8.4–6.8.6.

## 1.4 Conspectus

### 1.4.1 The applications

Some issues have traditionally been seen as more suitable for expert determination than others. The principal applications have been and remain rent review and share valuation, which are covered in Chapters 2 and 3. Chapter 4 considers the use of expert determination for the valuation of assets or liabilities transferred by agreements for the sale and purchase of businesses and companies. Chapter 5 reviews the remaining commercial applications. The transition from valuation to expert determination is considered in Chapter 6. Chapter 7 looks at industrial applications in the energy, mining, shipbuilding, construction and computer industries, where both valuation and technical skills of experts are used to settle issues.

### 1.4.2 Practice and procedure

The practical aspects of the subject, from drafting an 'expert clause' (see 1.1.4) through to enforcing a decision, are discussed in Chapters 8–12. Chapter 8 analyses the essential elements of an expert clause, applying the rules of contract law. Chapter 9 considers who can act as an expert: as the answer is anyone whom the parties appoint, safeguards are built into the expert clause to provide that a suitably qualified person is likely to act as the expert. Chapter 10 looks at the procedures for appointing experts, and in particular the role of professional bodies. Chapter 11 considers appropriate procedures for conducting a reference and Chapter 12 looks at the means of enforcing experts' decisions. Appendix A contains a series of precedents whose use is explained in the text of these chapters.

### 1.4.3 Contentious aspects

The most contentious aspects of expert determination are covered in Chapters 13–15. Chapter 13 explains the rule that the decisions of experts are final except in certain very limited circumstances. Chapter 14 deals with an expert's liability for professional negligence, and Chapter 15 explains the difference between experts and arbitrators.

### 1.4.4 Dispute resolution

Chapters 6, 16 and 17 discuss how expert determination is used as a method of dispute resolution. Chapter 6 looks at how expert determination is sometimes used alongside arbitration or litigation in the same contract, and considers the growing trend for its use for general, non-technical dispute resolution. Tactics in drafting agreements and conducting disputes are considered in Chapter 16: comparisons are made between litigation, arbitration, expert determination and alternative dispute resolution. Chapter 17 examines the court's policy in denying challenges to experts' decisions and considers the consequences of this policy in the context of the growing use of expert determination to resolve general disputes.

## 1.5 The predominant issues

### 1.5.1 How effective is expert determination?

Clients contemplating determination of an issue by an expert will wish to know whether a decision can be reached which will be final, and, if not, on what grounds they or the other party can mount a challenge; whether they can sue the expert; and whether they can avoid cost and formality.

### 1.5.2 Areas of contention remain

These issues continue to give rise to litigation. The desire of some parties for justice rather than finality fuels challenges to decisions; parties whose challenges fail wish to sue the expert; and the poorly defined boundary with arbitration provides material for disputes about disputes.

### 1.5.3 Challenging experts' decisions

Challenge is the most important of these issues. Chapter 13 identifies two key concepts in the law of challenge to experts' decisions:

(1) the law of contract; and
(2) mistake.

### 1.5.4  Primacy of contract law

The law of contract underpins expert determination: see especially 8.17 and 13.5.3. As a reference to an expert is a contract, disputes between the parties as to its validity have to be determined on that basis. The contracts typically say that the decision of the expert is to be final and binding, and that is what the courts say it has to be, in the absence of fraud, partiality or mistake.

### 1.5.5  Mistake

Disallowing an expert's decision on the ground of fraud or partiality is uncontroversial. It is mistake which causes problems. A mistake has to be fundamental to constitute a sufficiently serious breach of contract, such as the expert making his decision about the wrong subject-matter. Less serious mistakes are simply insufficient. Errors of fact or law will have to stand, provided the expert can be said to have asked himself 'the right question'.

### 1.5.6  'Construction' arguments

Challenges based on interpretation (or 'construction') arguments used to be effective: see an example at 7.2.4, where the court investigated the technology of oil fields in order to interpret the expert procedure. This would not happen now: recent changes in the law have made challenges on this ground virtually impossible after the decision has been made: see 13.9. Challenges on this ground can be made at an earlier stage in the reference by a construction summons, which is a procedure by which a party who disputes the meaning of a document can apply to the court for a ruling.

### 1.5.7  Can you sue an expert?

Chapter 14 shows how experts used to have immunity on the ground that they were some kind of arbitrator, until that immunity was swept away in 1975, but that it is still difficult to sue an expert. Despite those difficulties, it is still easier than proving that the expert has made a 'mistake' of sufficient gravity to invalidate the decision.

### 1.5.8　Arbitration

Disputes about whether a reference had been to an expert or an arbitrator have produced many lawsuits. The boundary between the two procedures is traced in Chapter 15. Recent changes in arbitration law may have the effect of discouraging these disputes.

## 1.6　The context of modern dispute resolution

### 1.6.1　Expert determination as dispute resolution

This book seeks to place expert determination in context with other forms of dispute resolution. There is no doubt that the procedure has now itself become a form of dispute resolution, but it must be distinguished from other forms of dispute resolution.

### 1.6.2　Not legal proceedings

First, references to experts are not legal proceedings. No court is involved unless there is a challenge. There is no statutory supervision by the court as there is with arbitration. A decision of an expert is not enforceable without court action.

### 1.6.3　Distinguish experts from expert witnesses

Secondly, expert determination should be distinguished from the use of expert witnesses in litigation and arbitration, which is such a dominant feature of modern dispute resolution. When a matter is referred to an expert for decision, he makes that decision himself. An expert witness is appointed by a party to assist in putting that party's case to a tribunal of either judge(s) or arbitrator(s), with other parties having the same right. In some European countries and in some international arbitrations, the tribunal appoints its own expert to advise on technical matters. While the evidence of an expert witness or the advice of a tribunal-appointed expert may have a decisive influence, it is the tribunal of judge(s) or arbitrator(s) which makes the decision as part of its judgment or award, and not the expert.

### 1.6.4　Expert determination, traditionally not dispute resolution

On one view, expert determination is not a form of dispute resolution at all. The argument depends on drawing a distinction between an 'issue' and a 'dispute' — or a 'formulated dispute'. Experts settle issues on which the parties have not taken defined positions: where the parties have taken defined positions, which become 'disputes' or '(formulated) disputes', the referee must be an arbitrator: see 15.5.

### 1.6.5 Share valuation: expert determines even where no dispute

Perhaps the only instances of expert determination where there is no dispute arise from the valuation of shares in private companies. The articles of association say that the value will be fixed by the company's auditors acting as experts and not as arbitrators, and there is no other way to arrive at the figure which follows the requirements of the constitution of the company. Even if the parties are in complete agreement on the issue, the auditors have to fix the value. Similar considerations arise where auditors certify the adjustment rates of convertible shares and the price of shares for employees in share option schemes.

### 1.6.6 Artificial distinction between 'issues' and 'disputes'

In all other cases it is artificial to draw this distinction between:
(1) 'issues' where the parties have not taken defined positions; and
(2) 'disputes' or 'formulated disputes' where the parties have taken defined positions.

If people have gone to the trouble and expense of referring something to a third party for decision, they are most likely not to have agreed about it, and however one analyses their disagreement, they are in dispute. The choice of reference, whether it is to be to expert or arbitrator, is in any event usually made at the time of the original contract which precedes the time when the parties know whether they have an 'issue to settle' or a 'formulated dispute', and they will be obliged to use whatever procedure was stipulated, unless they make some fresh agreement.

### 1.6.7 Development of expert determination into general dispute resolution

The fact is that parties to contracts do use expert determination for dispute resolution, and not only for certain types of disputes thought more suitable for experts: clauses referring all disputes, both technical and otherwise, are beginning to be found in contracts as a substitute for litigation or arbitration (see 6.9). This is part of a general trend towards simpler, cheaper and quicker forms of dispute resolution (see 16.6), and it may be the next stage of the history of expert determination. As Chapter 17 argues, it is a major issue of public policy.

# Chapter 2

# Land

## 2.1 Summary

This chapter deals with:
(1) the valuation of freehold land, including options (2.2);
(2) rent review (2.3);
(3) other leasehold valuations, including settling a price for long leases, compensation for surrender, options and service charges (2.4);
(4) the valuation of fittings, products and machinery associated with land (2.5).

### 2.1.1 Most traditional and important application

Land valuation is the most traditional application of expert determination, and rent review is now by far the most common instance of the procedure as applied to land valuation and, indeed, to any subject-matter.

### 2.1.2 Practical completion certificate cases

For cases where contracts for the sale or leasing of land are conditional on the issue of a practical completion certificate by an architect or similar construction professional, see 7.4.4.

## 2.2 Freeholds

### 2.2.1 Example of surveyor valuing development land in sale contract

Surveyors acting as experts sometimes decide the purchase price of land to be paid under contracts between vendor and purchaser. In *Campbell and Palmer v Crest Homes (Wessex) Ltd*

(1989) unreported, Chancery Division, 13 November, the plaintiff vendors agreed to sell some development land to the defendant purchasers at the price the property might reasonably be expected to fetch on the open market at the relevant date on a sale by a willing vendor to a willing purchaser; if the parties failed to agree the price within four weeks they were to refer to an independent surveyor to determine the price. The parties failed to agree and an independent surveyor, acting as an expert, determined the price. The purchasers failed in their challenge to the surveyor's valuation methods, and an order for specific performance of the expert's decision was made against them. The case raised issues of general principle which are discussed at 13.5.6 and 13.7.8.

### 2.2.2 Options to purchase successive plots

Surveyors acting as experts also decide the purchase price of freehold land subject to option agreements. A common application of this is the sale and purchase of successive adjacent plots over a period of time.

## 2.3 Rent review

### 2.3.1 Purpose of rent review clauses

A rent review is a procedure enabling a landlord and tenant to revise the amount of the rent payable under the terms of their lease to reflect changes in rental levels or circumstances: if they do not agree on the rental, the revision is referred to a third party. Thus, in a typical example, a commercial lease for a term of 25 years contains a covenant by the tenant to pay the rent under the lease. That covenant specifies the rent payable for the first five years. For each of the four succeeding periods of five years the covenant brings into operation the rent review provisions of the lease. The rent review provisions state that in the absence of agreement the review is to be conducted by the third party according to certain assumptions. The purpose of these assumptions is almost invariably to ensure that the new rent is a 'rack' rent, ie the highest commercially obtainable. The review is usually conducted by a surveyor, either as an expert or as an arbitrator. The rent review procedure is a useful means of enabling landlord and tenant to establish a long-term commitment, at a rental which continues, throughout that long term, to make commercial sense — especially during periods of inflation.

## 2.3.2 Standard forms include provision for rent reviewer to act as expert

There are two main standard forms of rent review clauses, from which most forms generally encountered derive. 'Model Forms of Rent Review Clause' has been produced jointly by the Law Society and the RICS. The current edition was published in 1985. It is reproduced in Bernstein and Reynolds. Precedent 1 provides for arbitration, precedent 2 for determination by an independent valuer (ie by an expert), and precedent 3 gives the landlord the right to choose whether the review is to be conducted by an expert or an arbitrator. Precedent 3, also known as 'Model Form — Variation C' is the most commonly used, and is reproduced at Appendix C. In all cases, if the landlord and the tenant are unable to agree on the identity of the rent reviewer, the RICS will make the appointment. The ISVA have also produced a standard form, published in 1984, and known as their 'Recommended Rent Review Clause'. The ISVA form provides for the review procedure to be by way of arbitration, unless the parties have already agreed on an expert. However, the ISVA will appoint an expert on application.

## 2.3.3 Assumptions, disregards and construction arguments

The standard forms of rent review clauses contain certain 'assumptions' and certain matters to be disregarded, known as 'disregards'. Model Form — Variation C lists the assumptions and disregards and can be studied at Appendix C. The principal assumption is an open market letting on the terms of the lease, and the principal disregard is the value of certain improvements. The interpretation of these provisions may provide material for 'construction' summonses where one of the parties asks the court to interpret the words used in the lease so that the rent review can proceed on the basis desired by the applicant. Very careful consideration is given to rent review clauses on construction summonses: for two recent examples see *Trust House Forte Albany Hotels Ltd v Daejan Investments Ltd (No 2)* [1988] NPC 59 and [1989] NPC 28, and *SB Property Co Ltd v The Chelsea Football and Athletic Company Ltd and Alexander Tatham and Co* [1990] NPC 86. In the *Trust House Forte* case the court had to interpret the assumption that premises were available for letting for shopping and retail purposes: the issue was whether the premises were to be taken as available for letting purposes only or whether they could be taken as to be available for letting for any other purpose permitted by the lease. The court chose the first of these two interpretations. The *Chelsea Football* case was about an unusual clause dealing with the calculation of the rent. Construction questions cannot be used as material for challenge to the determination after it has been made unless the expert has addressed the 'wrong question': see *Nikko Hotels (UK) Ltd v MEPC plc* [1991] 28 EG 86, discussed at 13.6.8. In the rent review context this has been said to mean that the court will tell surveyors what to value, but not how to value it: *Compton Group Ltd v Estates Gazette Ltd* (1977) 244 EG 799. For a robust rejection of forensic attacks on valuations by experts in rent reviews, see the words of Lord Templeman in *Hudson (A) Pty Ltd v Legal & General Life of Australia Ltd* [1986] 2 EGLR 130 quoted at 13.5.5.

### 2.3.4 Nikko v MEPC

*Nikko v MEPC* (cited at 2.3.3) applied the principles of *Jones v Sherwood Computer Services plc* [1991] NPC 60 (decided in 1989 and fully discussed at 13.6) to rent review cases. In *Nikko* an expert determined the 'average room rate' of a hotel as part of a rent review. The landlords said that the rate should be determined by reference to the published tariff. The tenants said that actual discounts given should be taken into account. The expert agreed with the landlords, and the tenants applied to the court to have the decision declared a nullity. The application was dismissed.

### 2.3.5 *Expert determination preferable to arbitration*

Bernstein and Reynolds give a very full treatment of the subject, much of which turns on the interpretation of provisions in commercial leases. Bernstein and Reynolds prefer rent reviews to be conducted as arbitrations, and that appears also to be the preference of the property community where the rent is substantial. This author believes that the expert procedure is better suited than arbitration to what is essentially a valuation exercise. The formal adversarial nature of arbitration produces some strange effects. Rent review arbitrations are unique in that the law allows the parties to the rent review to use subpoenas to force others with no other involvement in the affair to disclose the rental of buildings when that rental is the subject of a commercial confidentiality agreement: see the article by the author and Steven Dark in Further Reading. For a general comparison of litigation, arbitration and the expert procedure, see 16.3.

## 2.4 Other leasehold valuations

As well as rent review, other leasehold valuations include:
(1) the valuation of land held on long leases, as for instance in *Collier v Mason* (1858) 25 Beav 200;
(2) compensation for surrender, payable by the tenant to the landlord, where the tenant wishes to end the tenancy before the expiry of the term in the lease, and 'compensation for quitting', payable by the landlord to the tenant, where the landlord wishes to buy the tenant out. For a recent instance, see *Campbell v Edwards* [1976] 1 WLR 403, discussed at 13.5.3;
(3) options for tenants to purchase the freehold reversion; for an example, see *Sudbrook Trading Estate Ltd v Eggleton* [1983] AC 444, discussed at 10.3.3;
(4) service charges payable by the tenant certified by the lessor's surveyor: see *Re Davstone Estates Ltd's leases, Manprop Ltd v O'Dell* [1969] 2 Ch 378, discussed at 17.3.6.

## 2.5 Fittings, products and machinery

A number of cases have dealt with the valuation of fittings attached to or used in connection with land, whether freehold or leasehold, and associated products and machinery, whether in farms, public houses or factories: see:
(1) for a farming example, *Leeds v Burrows* (1810) 12 East 1, where the value of the outgoing tenant's hay and a 'spike-roll' had to be assessed;
(2) for a public house, *Smith v Peters* (1875) 2O LR Eq 511, where the household furniture, fixtures and other effects were to be valued; and
(3) for a factory, *Jones (M) v Jones (R R)* [1971] 1 WLR 840, where there was a small company carrying on a family business of manufacturing and retailing woollen goods, and there needed to be a valuation of the premises and the machinery.

# Chapter 3

# Shares in Private Companies

## 3.1 Summary

This chapter explains:
(1) the application of expert determination to the valuation of shares in private companies (3.2);
(2) that the procedure usually depends on the articles of association (3.3);
(3) that the experts are usually the company's auditors (3.4);
(4) the effect of the auditors being obliged to determine the 'fair value' of shares (3.5);
(5) the effect of specific valuation instructions (3.6);
(6) the special position where a minority shareholder petitions for winding-up (3.7).

## 3.2 Private companies

### 3.2.1 Shares not traded publicly

The valuation of shares in private companies is notoriously controversial, for the simple reason that the shares are not available for subscription by the public and their price is not quoted on a stock exchange. It is common commercial practice for the auditors of a private company to be called on to value the shares.

### 3.2.2 Occasions for transfer

Certain occasions dictate the compulsory transfer of the shares in a private company, such as the resignation of a director or other senior employee with a holding of the shares. Expert determination can be, and often is, also applied to voluntary transfer of shares or transmission of shares on the death of a shareholder.

### 3.3  Procedure depends on articles or shareholder agreements

*3.3.1  Valuation may otherwise be invalid*

The articles of association of each company, or, in some cases the shareholders' agreement, lay down the procedures for share valuation. (Articles of association are an agreement between the company and its members and between the members: Companies Act 1985, s 14.) The articles or the agreement may say that a reference to the auditors has to take place in every instance; in other cases a reference is necessary only if there is a dispute. If the articles or the agreement say that a reference is to take place in every instance, a reference there must be, even if there is no dispute between the shareholders about the value. If the shareholders agree on a value, and do not refer the matter to the company's auditors, their agreement and the ensuing transaction may be invalid because the price of the shares has not been established in accordance with the company's rules; and as a practical matter it might be unfair to other shareholders. If the value is not to be determined by the auditors, there has to be unanimous agreement of the shareholders. In other cases of non-compulsory transfer the parties will probably still be under the same constraints about fixing the price.

*3.3.2  Usual wording*

No standard forms for referring the valuation of shares in a private company to auditors as experts have been published. However, the auditors' task is usually expressed to be to state the 'fair price' of the shares; considered further at 3.5. A precedent is set out at Appendix D, showing typical provisions for valuations needed for a transfer.

*3.3.3  No representations*

These procedures are not framed in words which suggest that the determination is likely to be controversial. The parties are under no contractual obligation to allow each other to make representations to the auditor before he issues his certificate. For a discussion, see 8.15.

### 3.4  Appointment of a company's auditors

*3.4.1  Unusual features*

The words used say, almost invariably, that the auditors are to conduct the valuation, rather than an individual. This makes this

form of reference atypical for two reasons:
(1) the 'expert' is a group of individuals rather than one individual; and
(2) the identity of the 'expert' is known immediately, because every company must have auditors.

This is discussed further in Chapter 9.

### 3.4.2 Experts and not arbitrators

The words used also usually say that the auditors are to act as experts and not as arbitrators, and the commercial tradition is that they should not be arbitrators. For an instance where the court considered that auditors should be arbitrators, see 15.5.4, and for an example of an 'ad hoc' reference (defined at 8.2.4) of a share valuation dispute to an arbitrator, see *Harrison v Thompson* [1989] 1 WLR 1325.

### 3.4.3 Reasons for appointing auditors

There are said to be two reasons for referring the valuation of a company's shares to its auditors. The first is that they should be sufficiently familiar with the company's affairs already not to need to take further time to acquaint themselves with its business in order to provide the valuation. The second reason is that a company's auditors are expected, because of their statutory duties and position under the Companies Acts, to be independent of the shareholders in the company.

## 3.5 Fair value

### 3.5.1 Challenge on grounds that price is unfair

Questions have arisen as to whether the use of the word 'fair' as a characterisation of the price of the shares to be determined by the auditors makes their task any different and whether a valuation can be challenged on the ground that the price is not fair.

### 3.5.2 Baber v Kenwood

In *Baber v Kenwood Manufacturing Co Ltd and Whinney Murray & Co* [1978] 1 Lloyd's Rep 175, the auditors' task, following the wording of the company's articles of association, was to certify the 'fair selling value' of shares. The plaintiffs argued that the auditors had to use a basis of valuation which was capable of producing a figure which represented the fair selling value of the shares, and that if that basis were challenged, the court could decide whether the basis was such a basis. Megaw LJ said that each of the parties desired to avoid the possibility that the other might challenge the opinion of the valuer because the parties had stipulated that the auditors should act as experts, and by doing so they had showed that they wanted a measure of certainty, accepting the risk, which applied either way, that the expert might err. In other words, the test of fairness was whatever standard the auditors applied.

### 3.5.3 Reason for decision superseded, but same result today

Megaw LJ's argument depended on contrasting what would have happened if the auditors had been appointed as arbitrators. At that time (1978) there was a frequently used appeal procedure against arbitration awards. The procedure was known as 'case stated': it allowed appeals to the court on points of law, and sometimes resulted in an arbitration being followed by three further rounds of litigation in the High Court, the Court of Appeal and the House of Lords. Parliament decided that this was not what the parties to arbitration agreements either expected or wanted and abolished the case stated procedure by s1(1) of the Arbitration Act 1979: see further 15.8.3. The effect of the 1979 Act and subsequent case law is that arbitration awards have almost as great a degree of finality as experts' decisions, and so Megaw LJ's argument is no longer available. Faced with the same claims about the effect of words like 'fair', the courts today apply a doctrine of 'mistake' which precludes all review of the expert's analysis, unless the expert values the wrong shares or asks himself the wrong question about concepts such as fairness: see Chapter 13.

## 3.6 Specific valuation instructions

### 3.6.1 Minority holdings and going concerns

Sometimes the auditors are given more specific instructions about how they are to conduct the valuation. For instance, they may be directed, when valuing a minority holding of shares in a company, to value the shares without regard to the fact that the holding is a minority holding. The auditors may also be directed to value the shares on the basis that the company's business is a going concern, as opposed to a break-up basis.

### 3.6.2 Challenges on this ground

A successful challenge could be mounted on the basis that the auditors have not followed these instructions: for an example, see 13.5.2. But proving it may be difficult, especially where the auditors do not disclose their workings and calculations: see 13.7 on 'speaking' and 'non-speaking' decisions.

### 3.7 Unfair prejudice and minority holdings

A minority shareholder may override the transfer provisions in a company's Articles of Association by a successful application for an order under s 459 of the Companies Act 1985. This has been considered in a number of recent winding-up cases, notably in *Re Abbey Leisure Ltd* [1990] BCC 60, where the Court of Appeal said that two grounds for preferring a winding-up order to the transfer notice procedure and valuation by a company's auditor were:

(1) that there was nothing unreasonable in a petitioner with a minority holding refusing to accept a discount being applied to the valuation of his interest in the company, which an auditor was likely to decide on; and

(2) that there was machinery available in winding-up for the proper determination of claims, which was not available to an auditor.

In *Abbey Leisure* the transfer procedure was optional. In *Re a Company No 00330 of 1991 ex p Holden* [1991] BCC 241, the service of a transfer notice was a requirement imposed by the company's board under the Articles of Association. The judge in *Holden* upheld the petitioner's refusal to be bound by the transfer notice and granted his petition under s459.

Thus, in this instance, unusually in the subject of expert determination, contract may be displaced by statute.

# Chapter 4

# Sale and Purchase of Businesses and Companies

## 4.1 Summary

This chapter deals with the use of expert determination in agreements for the sale and purchase of businesses and companies, and, in particular:

(1) the certification of figures in accounts and the determination of issues such as net asset value (4.2);

(2) the determination by actuaries of the values of pension rights transferred (4.3); and

(3) the determination of tax liabilities (4.4).

## 4.2 Certificates of items in accounts

### 4.2.1 Establishing the amounts of deferred consideration

Agreements for the sale and purchase of shares in companies and the sale and purchase of businesses often provide that the amounts of the profits (or losses) of a company or business are to be certified by accountants. (For a precedent, see Appendix A). This is useful where, for instance:

(1) payment of part of the purchase price of a company or business is deferred, and

(2) the aggregate amount of the purchase price is itself dependent on the performance of the company or the business, over (typically) a one or two year period, or

(3) payment for the company or business is to be based on the net asset value stated in what are known as 'completion accounts' drawn up by accountants.

### 4.2.2 Breach of warranty

The expression 'breach of warranty' is often used in disputes about deferred consideration, when vendors are said in the agreement to 'warrant' that the profits reach a specified figure, and the purchasers seek a repayment from the vendors to compensate them for that loss, in most cases calculated on a pre-agreed formula: if the profits exceed the specified figure, the vendors may be entitled to additional consideration.

### 4.2.3 Issues for accountants

The issues accountants have to decide are the same whether the vendors are entitled to their deferred consideration or the purchasers are entitled to repayment of part of the purchase price because of breach of warranty. Very broadly, the accountants determine whether the right accounting methods have been used—for instance in dealing with such matters as rates of depreciation and work-in-progress. In certain cases, the accountants prepare the accounts of the company or business on predetermined bases or principles, which may be quite complex, and which will have been set out in the sale and purchase agreement. Often the vendors and the purchasers each appoint a firm of chartered accountants to act for them in determining the relevant amount and reference to a third accountant occurs only if the two firms cannot agree on that amount. If the parties' accountants agree on the figures without recourse to the third accountant their decision is still likely, depending on the words of the expert clause, to have the status of an independent decision: see 9.8.2 and *Shorrock Ltd v Meggitt plc* [1991] BCC 471, discussed in detail at 13.7.7. Another example of a breach of warranty claim is found in *Jones v Sherwood Computer Services plc* [1991] NPC 60, discussed in detail at 13.6.

### 4.2.4 Amounts commonly established

Amounts which are commonly established by accountants' certificates in sale and purchase of business agreements include:

(1) profits, losses and sales;
(2) the value of the stock;
(3) apportionments between vendor and purchaser;
(4) the turnover of service businesses and the value of service contracts;
(5) the evaluation of loan portfolios of banks;
(6) the net asset value of a company or business at a particular date; and
(7) the cost of repairing or replacing an asset transferred with the business.

Instances to have appeared in court cases are of accountants establishing net asset value and sales figures, in the examples in 4.2.3, and of accountants evaluating loan portfolios, cited at 4.4.

### 4.3 Pension schemes

#### 4.3.1 Transfer of pension rights

Sales of companies and businesses often include provision for the transfer of the pension rights of the employees concerned from the vendor's scheme to the purchaser's scheme. The transfer would, in a typical case, be achieved by a payment from the vendor's scheme to the purchaser's scheme and the provision by the purchaser's scheme of benefits of equal value to those provided by the vendor's scheme.

#### 4.3.2 Actuaries determine

It may be difficult or impossible to establish at the date of the sale the value of the pension rights to be transferred. Sale agreements commonly provide for the value of the pension rights to be calculated according to a formula set out in the agreement and for the detailed calculations to be agreed between the parties' actuaries, or, if they do not agree, to be determined by another actuary acting as an expert and not as an arbitrator. This application of the expert procedure is in fairly common usage.

#### 4.3.3 The Imperial Foods case

A challenge was made to an actuary's determination in *Imperial Foods Ltd's Pension Scheme* [1986] 1 WLR 717. A new pension scheme was to be set up after the sale of a business, and an actuary was to decide the portion of the funds from the old company's pension scheme to be set aside for the new company's scheme. The actuary had to choose between two different methods. The court upheld the actuary's choice. The court found that there was a wide division of opinion among actuaries as to the relative merits of both methods, that the method chosen by the actuary was a fair and proper method, and that the calculation based on that method was unobjectionable.

### 4.4 Tax liabilities

Tax liabilities in sale and purchase agreements are often determined by accountants acting as experts. An example is found in

*Royal Trust International Ltd v Nordbanken* (1989) unreported, Chancery Division, 13 October, where there was an agreement for the sale and purchase of a bank. Among the bank's assets were some loans of doubtful recoverability. If the loans were found to have been sold at a loss, the vendor would make a repayment, dependent on whether there had been a reduction in the bank's tax liability or not. That issue was referred by the sale and purchase agreement to a named firm of chartered accountants to determine as experts.

# Chapter 5

# Other Commercial Applications

## 5.1 Summary

This chapter considers various other commercial applications of expert determination, namely:
(1) employee remuneration and share options (5.2);
(2) partnership agreements (5.3);
(3) finance leasing (5.4);
(4) capital markets (5.5);
(5) convertible preference shares (5.6); and
(6) intellectual property (5.7).

## 5.2 Employee remuneration and share options

### 5.2.1 Remuneration

Under the provisions of a service agreement, an employee's salary, or a bonus, may be determined by the certificate of the company's auditors. This is quite common in practice, and appeared as the subject-matter of the dispute in *Johnston v Chestergate Hat Manufacturing Co Ltd* [1915] 2 Ch 338. In that case a clause in an agreement between a company and its manager stated that he should receive a fixed salary, and, as soon as the profits for the year had been ascertained and certified by the company's auditors, a percentage of 'the net profits (if any) of the company for the whole year'. The dispute turned on the calculation of the net profits.

### 5.2.2 Share options

The auditors may also be called upon to certify the adjustment of the option prices which employees are required to pay to acquire shares in companies under employee share schemes:

adjustment of the prices is necessary after capital reorganisation or rights issues.

## 5.3 Partnership agreements

### 5.3.1 Use of auditors' certificates

Partnership agreements often use auditors' certificates. For a modern example, see *Smith v Gale* [1974] 1 All ER 401, an unfortunate dispute in a small firm of solicitors. In that case the court found that the auditors' certificate was based on a mistaken interpretation of the agreement between the partners: this would probably not be decided the same way today: see 13.6, 13.7 and 13.9.

### 5.3.2 Extent of valuation exercise

What auditors have to do to determine the value of a partnership share may be, depending on the partnership agreement, either:

(1) simply to certify what the accounts say; or
(2) to make a much more complex investigation of the financial affairs of the partnership.

## 5.4 Finance leasing

### 5.4.1 Tax charges affecting rentals

Finance leases, which are similar to loans, often contain provisions for experts to determine variations in rental. Typically the customer selects the equipment from the supplier, and the finance lessor buys it and leases it to the customer on rentals calculated to pay off the purchase price plus interest. Unlike a lender, however, the lessor can claim capital allowances on the purchase price, normally at 25 per cent per annum of the reducing balance. Part of the lessor's cashflow benefit from the consequent reductions in his tax bill is passed on to the lessee by way of lower rentals, reducing the lessee's effective finance cost. A finance lease normally provides for rentals to vary should the lessor's cashflow not be as expected, for example if he fails to obtain the expected allowances or there is a change in the rate of tax. Leases may also provide for rental variations by reference to changes in interest rate.

*5.4.2*  Midland Montagu v Tyne & Wear

A recalculation of rentals after the 1984 reduction in corporation tax rates was considered in *Midland Montagu Leasing (UK) Ltd v Tyne & Wear Passenger Transport Executive and Ernst & Whinney* (1990) unreported, Chancery Division, 23 February. The court upheld the method (known as 'net after tax rate of return') used by the expert accountant as being common in the finance leasing business and envisaged by the parties. For a discussion of finance leasing, see Tolley's *Tax Planning 1991* Volume 2.

## 5.5  Capital markets

Another use of expert determination is found in the practice of the domestic and international capital markets. Trustees for the stockholders and eurobond holders are appointed under trust deeds. These trust deeds usually contain an expert clause about the remuneration of the trustee appointed under the deed. If there is a dispute about the fees, the matter is referred to a merchant bank to be resolved, with the president of the Law Society appointing the bank if the parties cannot agree on the choice of bank. For a precedent, see Appendix E. It is not thought that this procedure has been invoked with any degree of frequency.

## 5.6  Convertible preference shares

Expert determination is also used for the adjustment of the rate at which a convertible redeemable preference share is to be converted into, typically, an ordinary share, following a capital reorganisation or rights issue of the ordinary shares in the company. Under the relevant agreements, the directors usually make the adjustment, and if there is any doubt or dispute arising in respect of the adjustment the matter is referred to the auditors to certify an adjustment which is fair and reasonable in their view, to be binding on all concerned.

## 5.7  Intellectual property

*5.7.1  Royalties*

Intellectual property agreements, such as know-how licences, sometimes contain provisions referring questions about the level of royalties to an accountant, unless the issues are technical in which case they are referred to a patent agent.

### 5.7.2 Both commercial and industrial

Intellectual property applications of expert determination thus straddle the divide between commercial and industrial applications, discussed in the next two chapters.

Chapter 6

# From Valuer to Expert

## 6.1 Summary

This chapter examines:

(1) the remaining more traditional applications, commodities (6.2), legal questions (6.3) and insurance (6.4);

(2) how expert determination has been adapted and expanded by the notion that the referee is an 'expert' rather than a valuer (6.5), leading to new applications (6.6);

(3) the shift from deciding specific issues to resolving disputes (6.7);

(4) the use of expert determination alongside other forms of dispute resolution (6.8); and

(5) the use of expert determination as a form of general dispute resolution (6.9).

## 6.2 Commodities

### 6.2.1 Arbitration preferred to expert determination

Questions about the quality and price of commodities would seem to be natural applications for expert determination, but events have not borne out that assumption. In *Pappa v Rose* (1872) LR 7 CP 525 there was a dispute about the assessment by a commodity broker of the quality of 'Black Smyrna' raisins. The defendant, who had acted as selling broker between the plaintiff purchaser and the seller of the raisins, stated that the raisins were 'fair average quality of 1869 growth'. The plaintiff said the raisins were not within that quality definition, and that the broker had not exercised reasonable skill and proper care. The court held that the broker was in the position of an arbitrator, and therefore immune from liability: see further 14.3.1. Although expert determination would be entirely suitable, the tradition of the trade prefers arbitration and disputes of this sort are now generally referred to commodity arbitrations, discussed in 15.6.5.

### 6.2.2 Inspection certificates

However, some commodity contracts state that certificates of inspection of certain commodities are 'final' as to quality. The inspectors act as experts. The court has held that the certificates remain final, even though the inspector has been negligent, on the basis that they are no different from experts' decisions: *Alfred C Toepfer v Continental Grain Co* [1974] 1 Lloyd's Rep 11. Sometimes trade financing documents such as letters of credit require one of the parties to obtain the quality certificate of some internationally recognised body. While this sort of requirement is a condition precedent to the contract rather than an expert clause, the status of the certificate is the same as that of an expert's decision: see also 6.3.4.

### 6.3 Legal issues

### 6.3.1 Lawyers can act as experts

There is no reason why a legal issue should not be determined by a legal expert. It is a matter for the parties to decide how the lawyer should determine the issue, and the fact that a lawyer is to determine it does not mean that the procedure has to be an arbitration — a lawyer can act as an expert. The practice does not seem to be very common.

### 6.3.2 Evidence from nineteenth century cases

A dispute about a cheque was referred to counsel in *Boyd v Emmerson* (1834) 2 AD & E 183, and was held not to be an arbitration. In *Re Hammond & Waterton* (1890) 62 LT 808 the court said that if a building dispute were referred to an umpire who was a barrister the procedure would be more likely to be an arbitration, and that if the umpire were a quantity surveyor it would be more likely to be a valuation. (The court was explaining how to assess whether a procedure was an arbitration or a valuation: in that inquiry it might help to look at the profession of the umpire: see further 15.6.) The quote from *Hammond & Waterton* suggests that in 1890 it was thought that a barrister umpire could preside over a valuation: to restate the proposition in modern terms, a lawyer can act as an expert.

### 6.3.3 Leases to be settled by solicitor as expert

Property agreements sometimes state that the terms of conveyances or leases are to be agreed by the parties, or, if they fail to agree, will be settled by a solicitor specialising in real property of so many years qualification and practising in a particular locality, such as the City of London. These provisions are references to an expert.

### 6.3.4 QC clauses

Commercial agreements sometimes say that the opinion of a Queen's Counsel will determine whether and if so how a claim should proceed. Clauses of this type, often known as 'QC clauses', are encountered where litigation may need to be conducted in the name of or at the expense of another party, and that other party wants some assurance that the claim is sound. These clauses are also found in insurance policies to resolve disputes between insurer and insured as to whether a claim should proceed. The most well-known example is in the Solicitors' Indemnity Rules 1989, at General Condition 6.1.1 of Schedule 3 — the 'Master Policy' — covering the first layer of claims against all solicitors. It reads:

No Practice ... shall be required to contest any legal proceedings unless a Queen's Counsel (to be mutually agreed upon or failing agreement to be appointed by the President of the [Law] Society for the time being) shall advise that such proceedings should be contested.

These clauses, in the forms usually encountered, are more likely to be conditions precedent than true expert clauses, but the status of the opinion is the same as that of an expert's decision: see also 6.2.2 and 7.4.4.

### 6.3.5 Guarantees

Some on-demand guarantees contain clauses providing for one of the parties to certify an event such as a breach of contract triggering the guarantor's liability: see further 16.2.6.

### 6.3.6 Lawyer resolving general disputes

For the idea that a lawyer could be appointed to act as a legal expert to decide all types of disputes arising under a contract, see 6.9.3.

## 6.4  Insurance

### 6.4.1  Tharsis Sulphur v Loftus

Apportionment of cargo damage was referred to an average adjuster in *Tharsis Sulphur & Copper Co Ltd v Loftus* (1872) LR 8 CP 1, in circumstances where he appears to have determined the issue as an expert reference. However, the court decided, following the recent authority of *Pappa v Rose* (1872) LR 7 CP 525, that the average adjuster had the benefit of arbitral immunity. Lord Salmon's trenchant criticism of the *Tharsis* decision in *Sutcliffe v Thackrah* [1974] AC 727 is quoted at 15.5.2.

### 6.4.2  Arbitration preferred

For 'QC clauses' in insurance policies, see 6.3.4. Other examples of insurance claims being referred to experts do not appear in the reports and are not generally encountered in practice; the insurance world has a pronounced preference for arbitration.

## 6.5  Use of the word 'expert'

### 6.5.1  Original labels 'valuation' and 'appraisement'

The earlier cases do not generally talk about the referee as being an expert. If any descriptive word is used at all, it is usually 'valuer', and the procedure is called a 'valuation' or an 'appraisement', and not 'expert determination' or a 'reference to an expert'. The word 'experience' is used in some of the earlier cases to describe the necessary attribute of a valuer. For instance, in *Eads v Williams* (1854) 24 LJ Ch 531, arbitrators fixing the rent of a mine were said to be entrusted, from their *experience* and observation, to form a judgment, and therefore not to need to examine witnesses.

### 6.5.2  Appearance of the label 'expert'

The word 'expert' appears in the law reports with this meaning in *Bottomley v Ambler* (1878) 38 LT 545 where the following are found: 'you refer the matter to a person who is an expert as an expert . . .' and, confusingly '. . . in such a case, arbitrators, being experts . . .'. But 'valuer' is much more common at this time.

### 6.5.3  Appearance of formula 'as an expert and not as an arbitrator'

The first appearance in the law reports of the formula 'as an expert and not as an arbitrator' is in *Dean v Prince* [1953] Ch 590 at 591 (where it is misquoted) and, on appeal, [1954] 1 Ch 409 at 415. There an auditor was to certify the value of shares 'and in so certifying ... shall ... act as an expert and not as an arbitrator'.

## 6.6   New fields for experts

The twentieth century has seen the growth of new technologies and of the power of organised professions, which have assisted the expansion of the role of the referee from valuer to expert. The energy and computer industries are obvious examples. Applications of expert determination in the energy and computer industries are set out in Chapter 7. There are many new technologies, and the expert procedure may be appropriate to many more applications than the instances discussed in Chapter 7. The same changes in society have also been responsible for the parallel growth in the importance of experts acting as expert witnesses.

## 6.7   Dispute resolution

### 6.7.1   Experts closer to dispute resolution than valuers

Along with the development of the idea of the 'expert' there has been a trend towards the role of the expert being that of a dispute resolver. Surveyors, accountants and actuaries making valuations are often resolving disputes, but the disputes are limited to valuation issues. Leases and sale of business agreements often reserve specific issues to an expert; for instance, what the figure for sales should be in a particular set of accounts. In the more recently developed applications, expert clauses are less specific in that they do not reserve individual issues such as sales figures for determination by an expert, but refer general types of disputes to experts: for instance, 'all disputes of a technical nature arising under this agreement'. For traditional objections to the use of expert determination to resolve what are known as 'formulated disputes', see 15.5.

### 6.7.2   Contrasting use of experts who determine issues and expert witnesses

Dispute resolution now relies very heavily on expert witnesses for proof of technical issues. Expert witnesses should not be confused with expert determination: see 1.6.3. But there can be an overlap between the two. In a court case or arbitration where the only remaining issue is a matter of expertise, the parties can agree to refer that issue to an expert for determination. In *Capricorn Inks Pty Ltd v Lawter International (Australasia) Pty Ltd* [1989] 1 Qd R 8, the parties had settled the question of liability in their dispute and instructed a firm of accountants to act as experts to decide the amount of damages. Unfortunately one party increased its claim without notice to the other, which led to the court case discussed further at 13.13.2. The parties chose to refer the damages issue to a firm of accountants acting as experts in preference to litigation or arbitration. In both litigation and arbitration the parties would have had to use accountants as expert witnesses, with the judge or arbitrator deciding between them, on the basis of the expert witnesses' reports and their ability to withstand cross-examination. Either arbitration or litigation would have taken more time and cost more money than a successful reference to an expert.

### 6.7.3 Multi-party disputes

Great difficulty will be encountered in seeking to use expert determination outside a bipartite contractual dispute. Where there are third parties who need to be involved in resolving a dispute, expert determination will run into the same problems as multi-party disputes when attempts are made to submit them all to arbitration together: see Mustill and Boyd, pp 143–4. The problems arise because each agreement to refer is a separate contract, and each reference is private, so each of the parties concerned can insist on a separate reference excluding other parties. To solve the problem, either all the parties must co-operate after the dispute has arisen, which is inherently unlikely, or special clauses for the multi-party arrangements must have been drawn up and incorporated in each of the original contracts.

## 6.8 Two-tier dispute resolution

### 6.8.1 Getting the right forum?

Shipbuilding, construction and computer contracts considered in Chapter 7 use various types of 'two-tier dispute resolution'. Sometimes technical disputes are referred to an expert, while all other kinds of disputes go to arbitration or litigation: this may be useful in giving an appropriate forum of dispute resolution for whatever dispute arises.

### 6.8.2  Avoid disputes about the choice of forum

Questions, however, might arise about whether a dispute is a valuation/technical dispute to be referred to an expert or one that should be referred to an arbitral tribunal or the court. This will raise issues of interpretation of the disputes clause and an investigation of the type of dispute, which, unless some other provision is made in the contract, can be resolved only by the court if it has jurisdiction, or by arbitrators or a supervisory arbitral body, or possibly not at all. An awkward defendant could exploit this to the claimant's considerable disadvantage in time and money.

### 6.8.3  Solutions to this problem

One solution is a clause which says that the question of categorising disputes in contracts where there are two different modes of dispute resolution is itself to be referred to the expert for final decision. Another solution would be for the clause to say that disputes of a technical nature which the parties could not agree to refer to the expert should be referred to arbitration (or litigation) along with all other non-technical disputes.

### 6.8.4  Engineering contracts

Another type of two-tier dispute resolution is found in the traditional forms of engineering contracts, ICE and FIDIC. Here all disputes have first to be considered by the engineer who is the employer's agent: the engineer's function is to administer the contract and issue certificates and decisions in response to claims by the contractor for payment and claims of all kinds, such as claims for extensions of time in which to complete the works. The engineering contracts say that if disputes are not resolved by the engineer they have to be settled by arbitration. John Uff QC, writing in *Keating on Building Contracts* (at p 925), states that the engineer's decision is like that of a valuer. This creates an exception to both:

(1) the general practice that experts' decisions are final: see 8.8; and

(2) the less well-established principle that certifiers owe no duty of care to contractors: see 7.4.2.

Clause 66 of the sixth edition of the ICE contract has introduced a further tier of dispute resolution by interposing optional alternative dispute resolution (ADR) between the decision of the engineer and arbitration. The complexities are formidable, and may well create scope for disputes about the procedures themselves. The claimant must first refer his dispute to the engineer; if not settled, the dispute may then go to ADR, and, if it does go to ADR, and the conciliator makes a determination, it becomes binding unless one of the parties serves notice of arbitration within one month.

### 6.8.5    Adjudication

Similarly, in some modern construction contracts disputes are referred to 'adjudication' under which a named individual designated to act as an expert makes a preliminary finding which is then subject to review by arbitration. See the very full treatment by Mark McGaw in the article cited in Further Reading, where he sees adjudication as a species of expert determination.

### 6.8.6    Pre-arbitral expertise

The International Chamber of Commerce (ICC) have published 'Rules for Technical Expertise'. Under these rules, parties can agree to refer technical questions to one or more experts and seek a determination on an issue. Unless otherwise agreed, the findings of the expert(s) are not binding on the parties: they may be recommendations for the future performance of the contract. See the article by Michael Buhler cited in Further Reading.

## 6.9    Clauses referring all disputes to an expert

### 6.9.1    General dispute resolution

Clauses referring all disputes under a contract to an expert are encountered from time to time in practice. These clauses do not limit the exercise of the expert's judgment to valuation or technical questions, but call on him to act more like a judge or arbitrator. They have been found so far only in construction disputes, but there is nothing to prevent their use in other contexts. Clauses referring general disputes seem to choose individuals as experts, rather than firms or companies: see further 9.2.

### 6.9.2    Construction contract example

For instance, some building leases encountered in practice provide that 'any ... dispute ... in any way relating to the execution of the project shall be referred to the decision of an independent surveyor (acting as an expert and not as an arbitrator) ...'. This expert might have to deal with a wide variety of issues, including the builder's/lessor's obligations to obtain planning permission, as well as the design and construction obligations, issues which are usually left to an arbitrator or an Official Referee of the High Court.

### 6.9.3 Will the courts uphold these clauses?

Is it lawful to refer questions of fact and law to a third party to determine in a non-judicial fashion? An Australian case has explored this question: *Public Authorities Superannuation Board v Southern International Developments Corporation Pty Ltd* (1987) unreported (Smart J in Common Law Division of the Supreme Court of New South Wales, decision no 17896 of 1987, 19 October): cited by Burke and Chinkin in ICLR [1990] 443. The dispute was about a contract for the construction of a shopping centre complex in Sydney between parties referred to as the 'owner' and the 'developer'. The disputes clause referred disputes about 'any matter relating to the construction of the centre' under the contract to an engineering expert. The developer made a claim against the owner for extra costs caused by additional building works due to variations and initiated the reference of the claim to an expert. The owner tried to stop the dispute being decided by an expert. The owner said that the reference to a non-legal expert was inappropriate to a dispute about legal liability, and that despite the express words in the disputes clause in the contract, the parties could never have intended it. The owner objected to the process as well as to the qualifications of the expert: he insisted on litigation, and did not consider the possibility of appointing a legal expert. The court gave effect to this clause, stating that the parties should have considered the potential difficulties of using what the court called 'a single alternative dispute resolution process' for all disputes under the contract before making their contract. The court emphasised that it was upholding party autonomy and would not rewrite the contract to take account of subsequent concerns.

### 6.9.4 Public policy

For a discussion of the far-reaching consequences of the use of this type of clause, see Chapter 17.

### 6.9.5 Practical problems

There may be practical difficulties in finding an expert willing to accept an appointment to determine all disputes under a contract.

Determining all disputes is very likely to take an expert into matters that are outside his professional competence. An expert is liable for negligence (see Chapter 14) and he will enlarge the risk of his being sued if he decides matters not within his expertise.

Chapter 7

# Industrial Applications

## 7.1 Summary

This chapter considers the use of expert determination in:
(1) energy and mining contracts (7.2);
(2) shipbuilding contracts (7.3);
(3) construction contracts (7.4);
(4) computer contracts (7.5);
which display the following features discussed in Chapter 6:
(5) the use of technical experts drawing on expertise not directly associated with valuation;
(6) the use of technical experts to act as general dispute resolvers; and
(7) the use of 'two-tier' dispute resolution procedures.

## 7.2 Energy and mining

### 7.2.1 Oil and gas agreements

Commercial agreements in the oil and gas industries use expert determination in the following three ways. The first relates to the pricing of oil and gas supplies, the second to apportioning costs and entitlements in unitised oil and gas fields and the third to the construction of facilities. (For an explanation of unitisation, see 7.2.3). This section looks at the first two of these applications. Construction applications are covered in 7.4.

### 7.2.2 Fixing the price

Gas supply agreements often provide for the supply of gas over a long period, sometimes for a decade or more. It used to be common for agreements for the supply of crude oil to do the same, but these have gone out of fashion in recent years with the volatility of oil prices: they may reappear if the oil price settles down. In long-term supply agreements it is desirable to have some agreed method for fixing the price, either on a quarterly or on a cargo by cargo basis. Agreements often specify 'market price'. In some cases 'market price' may be defined in relatively simple terms, such as by reference to the price quoted in a recognised trade journal. In other cases, a formula may be spelled out in the agreement showing how the market price is to be established. This formula can sometimes be quite detailed. If the parties cannot agree on the price according to the formula, the matter is referred to an expert in the market.

### 7.2.3 'Unitised' projects

Apportioning costs and entitlements in an oil or gas field is often necessary to settle matters between the participants in a unitised project. In a unitised project, persons having differing interests in two or more different areas or 'tracts' agree that a field underlying their respective tracts should be developed and produced as one project. The exact proportions in which oil and/or gas is present in the respective tracts become fully apparent only as wells are drilled in the course of operations. By a process known as 'redetermination of equities', the interested parties agree that the proportion which their respective stakes bear to one another is to be reassessed after a certain period, or at periodic intervals. When the final redetermination is made, the nature and extent of the oil and/or gas field and the amount of the oil and/or gas present in each of the tracts should be more apparent as a result of the drilling and production. The assessment of the relative 'equities' of the parties depends on an understanding of the geology of the site and the engineering technicalities of extracting the oil and/or gas, and the application to that information of an agreed method of calculation. If the parties are unable to agree on the precise application of the method of calculation to the information derived from the drilling and production, the dispute may be referred by the agreement to an expert to determine.

### 7.2.4 Arco v Sun Oil

The court reviewed an agreement of this type in *Arco British Ltd v Sun Oil Britain Ltd* (1988) unreported, Court of Appeal, 14 December. The method of redetermination employed by the experts was challenged as a matter of interpretation of the words of the agreement. The court investigated the technology in some detail, but stressed that it was not evaluating the experts' decision, just construing the words of the agreement. The parties accepted that the court was entitled to decide matters of construction because, as well as the clause in their agreement providing for expert determination, there was also a clause which said that the agreement was to be governed and construed in accordance with the laws of England and that the parties submitted to the jurisdiction of the High Court. The judgment in *Arco* preceded *Jones v Sherwood Computer Services plc* [1991] NPC 60, (decided in December 1989) which, as now applied in *Nikko Hotels (UK) Ltd v MEPC plc* [1991] 28 EG 86, precludes review by the court of the expert's interpretation of the material at issue. Although questions of interpretation are traditionally questions of law the court will intervene only if the expert has asked himself the 'wrong question': see 13.6.8, 13.8 and 13.9. Allegations that the expert has made a mistake will succeed only if the mistake is an error so fundamental that no expert is likely to have made it.

### 7.2.5 Electricity

Expert determination is also used in electricity supply contracts, which are not strictly supply contracts but contracts for differences, because the electricity is supplied from a pool and the purpose of the contract is to cover price fluctuations. Experts are used in electricity contracts to determine technical issues and/or the price.

### 7.2.6 Mining

Disputes about the price and quality of metals are usually referred to arbitrators under the rules of the London Metal Exchange: for commodity arbitrations, see 15.6.5. Long-term contracts for the supply of uranium have contained expert clauses for determining the price of the concentrate.

## 7.3 Shipbuilding

### 7.3.1 Technical question may go to an expert but still be reviewable

Shipbuilding contracts often provide that technical disputes about the construction of a ship and the materials and workmanship are to be referred to an expert for determination. Whether the reference to an expert takes place may be subject to the agreement of the parties to the shipbuilding contract. If the parties do not agree on the reference, they will still be able to pursue the matter through arbitration or litigation.

### 7.3.2 *In other contracts expert's decision is final*

Some contracts refer technical disputes to an expert whose decision is final and binding. An example is Art 15(*b*) of the standard form of shipbuilding contract adopted by the Association of West European Shipbuilders, reprinted in *Shipbuilding Contracts* by Malcolm Clarke (Lloyd's of London Press Ltd, 1982).

### 7.3.3 *Classification Societies*

In practice, experts are rarely appointed to determine issues under shipbuilding contracts, because of the role played by Classification Societies. Member bodies of the International Association of Classification Societies are independent bodies of marine surveyors recognised by governments throughout the world as their agents for the implementation of the international maritime safety conventions. One of the best known Classification Societies is Lloyd's Register of Shipping, based in London.

### 7.3.4 *Effect of requirement of compliance with rules of Classification Society*

Shipbuilding contracts invariably say that the ship must comply with the rules of the relevant Classification Society. Thus in practice the role of a Classification Society enables many of the differences of opinion between a builder and an owner about the construction of a ship to be settled without formal recourse to an expert. Where differences remain, a Classification Society might be seen as an ideal expert to decide technical disputes about the construction of ships. However, because a Society is usually engaged by the builder during construction and the owner following delivery, the commercial conflict of interest generally rules this out. For example, Lloyd's Register surveyors invariably decline to be nominated as experts to determine technical disputes during construction, for this very reason; and the parties usually refer disputes to arbitration rather than expert determination.

*7.3.5 Classification Societies as experts?*

Some would say that the result is that a Classification Society does act as an expert in resolving technical disputes. Non-classification technical disputes rarely occur, and when they do, the trade preference is for arbitration.

## 7.4 Construction

*7.4.1 Use of experts in construction contracts*

Experts are appointed under construction contracts for two purposes: first, to determine valuation or technical questions; or, second, to decide all disputes under the contract. A recent example of the first category appeared in a contract for the construction of offshore oil exploration facilities in the North Sea—technical disputes about whether the work or the facilities complied with the contract were to be referred to an expert. For examples of the second category, see 6.9. An expert appointed to resolve all disputes under a construction contract will need to be given the powers of an arbitrator to review certificates issued under the contract, because an expert would not have those powers any more than the court does, unless the parties agree: *Northern Regional Health Authority v Derek Crouch Construction Co Ltd* [1984] 1 QB 644, and 8.4.3.

*7.4.2 Certification*

Certification under construction contracts should be distinguished from expert determination. Architects, engineers and other construction professionals certify amounts due from the owner to the contractor under construction contracts. They usually act as the employer's agent, and therefore have a dual function; as well as giving the contractor instructions, the certifier administers the contract. It is administration, rather than deciding issues or resolving disputes, even though the certifier often has to accept or reject claims by the contractor as to what he should certify for payment. The courts used to see this certifying role as 'quasi-arbitral', giving the certifier a very similar status to that of an expert, with the result that the certifier could not be sued for negligence. This line of authorities was overruled by the House of Lords in *Sutcliffe v Thackrah* [1974] AC 727: see 14.4. The Lords went on, in *Arenson v Casson Beckman Rutley & Co* [1975] 3 WLR 815, a case about auditors valuing shares in a private company, to abolish the immunity of experts as well. An expert can be liable in contract or tort to both the parties who have referred an issue to him for decision: see 14.5 — 14.11. However, a certifier is liable only to his client the employer and not to the contractor: see *Pacific Associates v Baxter* [1990] QB 993. In that case the contractor sought to sue the engineer for losses arising from alleged under-certification of the amounts due to the contractor. The engineer was the client of the employer. The court struck out the contractor's claim. See further Sir Anthony May in *Keating on Building Contracts*, pp 113–14.

### 7.4.3   Certification usually interim

Certificates are decisions of the employer's agent: in the forms of contract usually encountered, the certificates are reviewable by arbitration. This is the position even with the special machinery under the ICE and FIDIC contracts, where disputes have first to be referred to the engineer. If the claimant is still dissatisfied, the dispute goes to arbitration, where the engineer's decision can be reviewed. However, sometimes the decision of the certifier is not reviewable in that way, as, for instance, in the construction management contract dispute *Beaufort House Development Ltd v Zimmcor (International) Inc* (1990) 50 BLR 91. In that case it was argued, unsuccessfully, that the construction manager's decision was final and binding as a valuation. Similar unsuccessful arguments have been raised in other construction cases where a dispute has halted a contractor's or subcontractor's cash flow. In any case, the status of a valuation produced by a person who is the agent of one of the parties only can be a fertile source of argument, as can be seen from *Panamena Europea Navigacion (Compania Limitada) v Frederick Leyland & Co Ltd (J Russell & Co)* [1947] AC 428.

### 7.4.4   Practical completion 'triggers'

One application of expert determination where the expert is the agent of one party only is in land transactions between vendor and purchaser or landlord and tenant. The completion date for the purchase of the land or the date when rent starts to be payable by the tenant is triggered by the issue of the certificate of practical completion of the building being bought or leased. (This machinery is similar to the condition precedent cases at 6.2.2 and 6.3.4.) The certificate of practical completion is issued by the architect (or other construction professional) who is the agent of the vendor and acting as certifier in the separate contract for the

construction of the building being sold or let. In *Bridger Properties Ltd v Dovey Holdings (South Wales) Ltd* (1991) unreported,
Chancery Division, 25 June there was a contract for the sale of
land with a completion date 14 days after the issue of the certificate for practical completion. The purchaser did not accept that
the building was in a state of practical completion and refused to
complete. The contract did not say that the architect was acting as
an expert, nor that his decision would be final and binding. The
court rejected the 'uncommercial' suggestion that the reference,
to achieve those results, would have had to have been to arbitration, and held that it was irrelevant whether the architect
issued his certificate mistakenly, because both parties had taken
the risk he might do that.

### 7.4.5   Tortious liability for issuing practical completion
certificate

Would the issuer of a practical completion certificate be potentially liable for the tort of negligence to the purchaser? If the
issuer did not know that the issue of the certificate triggered
completion of the sale, or that it would be likely to do so, he
would probably not be liable: see 14.11.

### 7.4.6   Confusion over the word 'certificate'

The expression 'certificate' and its cognates can cause confusion
between the construction industry usage and the wordings found
in expert accountant clauses, where the word 'certificate' means
the decision of the expert. The context and the tradition are
different. The usages in cases like *Bridger v Dovey* result in the
word 'certificate' being used to mean both simultaneously.

### 7.4.7   Adjudication

The use of adjudication in construction contracts is discussed at
6.8.5.

## 7.5   Computers

Computer contracts sometimes provide for experts to determine technical issues such as whether the computer equipment or
software performs in accordance with its specification, or the
interpretation of specifications or other related technical docu-
mentation. No instance has yet reached a reported court case.

# Chapter 8

# The Expert Clause

## 8.1 Summary

This chapter:
(1) explains the need to specify expert determination to ensure it will be applied (8.2);
(2) lists the elements of an expert clause (8.3);
(3) analyses each of those elements (8.4–8.16); and
(4) shows how the court interprets badly drafted expert clauses (8.17).

The chapter should be read in conjunction with the precedent at Appendix A1.

## 8.2 Need to specify expert determination

### 8.2.1 Prior agreement necessary

Expert determination must be expressly specified in the agreement. If the parties to an agreement want to refer their disputes to an expert and to keep the dispute out of court, they must say so specifically in the agreement. Only that sort of provision will bind the parties in advance.

### 8.2.2 The 'expert clause'

In every contract where expert determination is to be used, there will be a clause which refers questions arising under the contract to an expert and which contains a number of ancillary provisions. In this book this clause is referred to as the 'expert clause'.

### 8.2.3 Incorporation of expert determination

The manner in which expert determination is incorporated into the agreement depends on the type of reference contemplated.

Here are some examples:

(1) Articles of association of a private company may say that the share price on a compulsory transfer is to be certified by the auditors.

(2) An agreement for the sale and purchase of a business may reserve a number of issues to expert determination, such as the profits figure for a company or the net asset value of a business: see the full list set out at 4.2.5. Those issues appear in various parts of the agreement, and expert determination is applied to those issues by one expert clause. The expert clause specifically refers to those other clauses and states that expert determination is to be applied to issues arising under them.

(3) A construction contract may provide for the determination by an expert of technical issues in a disputes clause providing for arbitration of non-technical issues: see 6.8.

(4) The disputes clause of a construction contract may refer general disputes to an expert for determination: see 6.9.

This book uses the expression 'expert clause' to refer to all of these types of clause.

### 8.2.4 *Agreements to refer after a dispute has arisen*

There is nothing to stop the parties agreeing, after a dispute has arisen, to refer their dispute to an expert for his determination, and this is done from time to time, in the same way as arbitration agreements. For a recent example, see *Capricorn Inks Pty Ltd v Lawter International (Australasia) Pty Ltd* [1989] 1 Qd R 8, where a dispute about damages was referred to accountants by an agreement entered into after the parties' dispute about liability had been settled by some other method; there had been no prior agreement in the original contract to refer to an expert. The same law and the same rules of construction apply both to clauses in agreements entered into before a dispute has arisen and subsequent agreements to refer entered into after a dispute has arisen. The latter are sometimes known as 'ad hoc' references.

### 8.2.5 *Difficulties with oral agreements*

An agreement to refer an issue to an expert need not be in writing, but modern commercial practice will ensure that oral agreements for expert determination are most unlikely. People are likely to create at least one piece of paper when making an agreement of sufficient complexity to incorporate expert determination. In any case, the problems of proving the terms of an oral agreement can be insurmountable.

## 8.3   Essential elements of an expert clause

Expert clauses should contain the items in this list, which also shows where to find discussion in the text and wording in the precedent at Appendix A1:

- the issue to be determined (8.4) (1.1);
- the expert's qualifications (8.5) (1.1);
- that he is to act as an expert and not as an arbitrator (8.6) (1.3);
- how the expert is to be appointed (8.7) (1.1);
- that the decision will be final and binding (8.8) (1.3);
- the due date for payment of the amount determined (8.9) (1.3);
- that the expert has the power to award interest (8.10) (1.3);
- provision for interest to run for late payment of the amount determined (8.11) (1.4) (sometimes found elsewhere in the agreement); and
- how the expert is to be paid (8.12) (1.3).

Sometimes the following are useful:

- provision for awarding costs between the parties (8.13);
- provision where one party does not pay the expert's fees (8.14);
- procedure for the actual reference (8.15) (1.2); and
- time bars (8.16).

## 8.4   The issue to be determined

### 8.4.1   Are there precedents available?

Where the issue to be determined falls into one of the categories discussed in Chapters 2–7, a precedent can be found. Where the issue does not fall into a familiar category, there may be more scope for the draftsman.

### 8.4.2   Importance of clear definition

Unless the expert is determining all disputes under a contract (see 6.9), it is vital to define the issue clearly to avoid disputes about the interpretation of the words. The expert's jurisdiction to make a determination depends on the definition of the issue between the parties. It may suit one of the parties at the time of the reference to exploit the uncertainty created by poor drafting, either by delaying matters by a construction summons (see 8.17.7) or by insisting on a particular definition of the issue which is to that party's advantage. For difficulties with 'two-tier' dispute resolution, see 6.8.

### 8.4.3 Special powers for expert resolving construction disputes

Where an expert is resolving disputes under a construction contract he will need to be given the powers of an arbitrator to review certificates issued under the contract by the architect or engineer. In *Northern Regional Health Authority v Crouch* [1984] 1 QB 644, the Court of Appeal held that the court does not have the powers of an arbitrator under standard form construction contracts to 'open up, review, and revise any certificate, opinion, decision, requisition or notice ... and to determine all matters in dispute ...'. An expert must therefore be given these powers by the expert clause; otherwise his jurisdiction will be severely limited.

### 8.5 The expert's qualifications

The clause will establish, conclusively, what qualifications the expert is supposed to have. It is therefore most important to provide for this in the expert clause. This is usually taken care of by stipulating an appointing authority. Appointing authorities have reputations to keep and therefore have an incentive to maintain standards. It is also usual to specify a professional qualification. For a full discussion, see Chapter 9.

### 8.6 To act as an expert and not as an arbitrator

#### 8.6.1 The favourite wording

The most commonly encountered wording is that the referee is to act as an expert and not as an arbitrator. That wording is much more common than one which merely says that the referee is to act as an expert, omitting 'and not as an arbitrator'. It is not clear whether it makes any difference if those words are omitted. Probably the extra words are left in by most draftsmen because of understandable caution.

#### 8.6.2 Serious consequences of omitting these words

Failure to use these words can lead to a lot of confusion, and provide opportunities for awkward parties to obstruct a reference by questioning the procedure used to arrive at a result which they expect to be unfavourable. This can be seen from the cases reviewed in Chapter 15: and see especially 15.3.

### 8.7 How the expert is to be appointed

#### 8.7.1 By agreement

If the expert's identity is not predetermined by, for instance, being the company's auditors, the expert clause should say that the expert is to be appointed by agreement of the parties.

#### 8.7.2 By a professional body

The clause must also deal with how the expert is to be appointed if the parties cannot agree on his appointment, usually with the help of a professional body: see 10.2.

#### 8.7.3 Avoid the requirement for joint applications

Difficulties sometimes arise when one of the parties refuses to join the other party in applying to the designated appointing authority to appoint an expert. This can be solved by a provision enabling either one of the parties to apply on its own. Without that provision, either the appointing authority will have to be persuaded to act and the other party persuaded to drop its objections, or an application would have to be made to the court for a declaration as to whether the reference should proceed.

#### 8.7.4 Replacement experts

Sometimes provision is made for appointing a replacement expert. So far no case has reached the reports where there has been difficulty because of the death, retirement or other incapacity of an expert after appointment. It may be as well to provide for the eventuality. The court cannot be relied on to imply a term that the parties should co-operate in the appointment of a replacement: see 8.17.4.

### 8.8 That the decision will be final and binding

#### 8.8.1 Is there any difference between 'final' and 'binding'?

Expert clauses very commonly provide that the decision will be final and binding, and it is clearly in the parties' interests that it should be so. Is there any difference between 'final' and 'binding'? 'Final' means that the decision is not subject to review, and 'binding' means that the parties are obliged to comply with the decision. Therefore 'final and binding' is not tautologous, and the wise draftsman will put both words into the clause to preclude arguments later.

### 8.8.2  Would the court imply the term?

It is likely that the court would imply a term that an expert's decision is both final and/or binding (see 8.17.5), but the party seeking to establish that might face the cost and uncertainty of litigation.

### 8.8.3  Interim decisions in construction contracts

In some construction contracts the decision of the engineer or adjudicator may be that of an expert but still be reviewable by arbitration and therefore not final, although it will be binding until it is reviewed by arbitration: see 6.8.4.

### 8.8.4  Effect of certain qualifying words

Sometimes the finality of the decision is expressed to be subject to the qualification 'save in the case of manifest error'. These words probably do not enlarge the scope for challenge: see 13.11.

### 8.8.5  Conclusiveness

For a discussion of the concept of the conclusiveness of an expert's decision, see 13.7.7.

## 8.9  The due date for payment of the amount determined

It is useful to specify the due date for payment of the amount determined by the expert. A provision of this sort does not have to be included in every decision because it may be implied in the issue referred and the underlying contract under which the reference is made. The obvious example is rent review, where the date for payment of the revised rent is found in the lease, provided it has been properly drafted. But other expert clauses may well need this provision to prevent arguments about when the amount is payable: 14 days from the date of publication of the decision is the usual period.

## 8.10  That the expert has the power to award interest

### 8.10.1  No implied power

The expert does not have the power to award interest unless the contract says so. There is a doctrine that an arbitrator whose task is to declare an amount payable, rather than award damages, or an expert performing a similar role, does not have the power to award interest: *Knibb v National Coal Board* [1987] QB 906. This still appears to be the case despite the enactment of s 19A of the Arbitration Act 1950, which gives arbitrators the statutory power to award interest. Thus, when in *Trusthouse Forte Albany Hotels Ltd v Daejan Investments Ltd (No 1)* [1980] 256 EG 915 the lease under which the rent reviewer was acting as an expert did not provide for interest to compensate the landlord for the tenant's delay in paying the increased rent, the court refused to imply the missing term.

### 8.10.2  Cases where power is needed

The need to ensure that the expert has the power to award interest will arise in the following circumstances:

(1) Does the issue referred to the expert include a claim for damages arising from some breach of contract that has already occurred?

(2) Is the issue the expert is called on to determine essentially what amount of money one side owes the other, and when that sum is payable?

(3) Is there likely to be a delay in obtaining the expert's decision on the amount payable?

These circumstances will arise in the majority of instances of expert determination.

### 8.10.3  Rent reviews

For rent reviews, commercial leases contain their own machinery for dealing with this problem, because the new rental decided by the expert becomes the rent as defined in the lease, and the landlord's rights to the rent and interest on late payment are generally as full as the law permits—with penal rates of interest for delay. However, many other agreements incorporating expert determination do not have this sort of machinery.

### 8.10.4  Attractions of delay to party ultimately liable

The likelihood of delay should not be underestimated. The party ultimately having to make a payment will look for ways to postpone that event for as long as possible, and will be able to do so without risk if there is no interest provision.

### 8.10.5 Tactics

As well as simple tactics like tardiness in dealing with corre-spondence, construction summonses can cause significant delay: see 8.17.1 and 8.17.7.

### 8.10.6 Rate of interest

The appropriate rate of interest to compensate for delay during the determination process is 1 per cent over base.

## 8.11 Provision for interest to run for late payment of the amount determined

Clauses often provide that the amount determined by the expert is payable within 14 days of the publication of the decision. There needs to be some method of ensuring that interest compen-sates for delay after this date. Usually the expert clause does not give the expert the right to award this interest: it is provided elsewhere in the agreement as an obligation arising between the parties. Here the rate of interest can be as high as 4 per cent over base.

## 8.12 How the expert is to be paid

The clause may often say that the expert's fees are to be borne equally, or in agreed proportions, by the parties, or wholly by one of the parties, or as the expert may direct, or, for instance in the case of share valuation, that the fees are to be borne by the company. Or the clause may not say how they are to be paid, in which case this should be covered at the time of fixing the pro-cedure. Sometimes clauses make similar provision for the expert's expenses as well as his fees. By contrast, advance apportionment of costs before a dispute has arisen is illegal in arbitrations: s 18(3) of the Arbitration Act 1950.

## 8.13 Provision for awarding costs between the parties

### 8.13.1 Liability for costs could deter frivolous references

The expert will not have the power to award costs between the parties unless the clause says so. In arbitration as well as litiga-tion, the tribunal has a discretionary power to order the payment of costs between the parties: usually the loser has to pay the winner's costs. Giving the expert a similar power could be valuable in deterring frivolous references. It would almost certainly not be obtainable by negotiation later than this stage.

### 8.13.2 No 'taxation' machinery available

In litigation and arbitration, the amount of the costs is subject to the control of the court's 'taxation' procedures, which are made available to arbitrations by s 18(2) of the Arbitration Act 1950, but cannot be made available for expert determinations by any means, including a provision to that effect in the expert clause.

## 8.14 Provision where one party does not pay the expert's fees

It may be useful to say what is to be done if one party does not pay his share of the expert's fees. The Model Forms of Rent Review Clause contain a provision entitling the other party to pay the expert's fees in full and then reclaim the balance from the non-paying party as a debt payable on demand.

## 8.15 The procedure to be followed in the reference

### 8.15.1 The right to make representations

Expert clauses take various approaches to the question of whether the procedure the expert is to follow in the reference should be set out in the expert clause. Some clauses say that the parties have the right to make 'representations' or 'submissions', whereas others do not. These expressions do not mean that the parties have the right to be heard at a formal hearing: what they convey is that the parties can state their case in writing.

### 8.15.2 No right in certain company applications

For instance, in the commercial applications, the articles of association of a company do not specify a procedure, but merely say that the auditors are to certify the value of the shares (see Chapter 3): the same brevity is encountered in the share option (5.2) and convertible preference share examples (5.6). This suggests that the draftsman did not expect there to be controversies; all that would happen would be the consideration of the issue by the expert and the publication of his determination. In the second and third examples, it also reflects the practical difficulties of the potentially very large number of parties affected who might want to make representations.

### 8.15.3 Sale of businesses

In cases where accountants determine matters such as the net asset value of a business which has been transferred (see Chapter 4), the expert clauses sometimes specify that the parties can make representations, but may be reticent on the point.

### 8.15.4 Rent reviews

The Model Forms of Rent Review Clause say that both the landlord and the tenant will have the chance to make representations to the valuer.

### 8.15.5 Dispute resolution

However, in cases where all technical disputes are referred to an expert for determination, and those where all disputes, technical and non-technical are referred, it is uncommon to find provisions allowing the parties to make representations to the expert. Whether this reflects poor drafting or a more leisurely attitude to the question of the right to make representations is unclear.

### 8.15.6 Right to make representations should be in expert clause

It may be of some importance to provide in the expert clause that the parties have the right to make representations. If that right is not set out in the expert clause the agreement of the parties (and, probably, the agreement of the expert as well) will be needed for it to become part of the reference.

### 8.15.7 Should details of the procedure be set out in the expert clause?

Expert clauses which set out the procedure in more detail than providing that the parties have the right to make representations are probably not very helpful. There is no reason why the clause should not set out the detail of the procedure, such as time limits by which representations have to be made, and whether representations are to be exchanged simultaneously between the parties or served consecutively like pleadings. But if there is a clear road to the appointment of a suitable expert, it should be safe to leave the details of the procedure to be settled after his appointment. This will hold good for the more regularly used applications.

### 8.15.8 It may be an advantage in some cases

There may be an advantage in laying down a procedure where the application is novel, and/or the parties believe that a particular approach is necessary and that if it is not stipulated an expert is likely to follow some other undesired procedure. For instance, if the parties do not want the expert to consider any evidence other than that contained in their submissions, and do not want him to make his own independent investigations, they could stipulate to that effect in the expert clause. See further 14.8.

### 8.15.9 Obligation to provide information

The implied duty to co-operate (see 8.17.4) should make it unnecessary to stipulate that the parties will provide the expert with all information and documents he reasonably requires: sometimes expert clauses contain a specific provision to this effect.

### 8.15.10 Confidential documents

The part of the procedure that it may in some cases be desirable to include will be a provision that the parties will disclose confidential documents or authorise production of documents by a third party; see clause 2 of precedent 1 in Appendix A.

## 8.16 Time bars

### 8.16.1 Time bars may prevent references to an expert

Commercial contracts often contain time bars which seek to prevent claims after a specified date. They may be used to prevent a reference to an expert after that date, in which case an existing determination, made by or on behalf of one of the parties but not accepted by the other, may have to stand.

### 8.16.2 Interpreted to give benefit of doubt to party adversely affected

These time bars are clauses whose purpose and effect is to restrict or exclude liability. Their wording is therefore interpreted with the benefit of any doubt given to the party adversely affected: see *Chitty on Contracts*, Chapter 14.

### 8.16.3 Unfair Contract Terms Act 1977

Time bars may be subject to the requirement of reasonableness in ss 2 and 3 of the Unfair Contract Terms Act 1977. Where, however, they are found in a specially negotiated contract between two companies, the court is unlikely to have sympathy for the party who has missed the deadline.

### 8.16.4 No machinery for extending time

There is no machinery for extending the period for claims, as there is with late notices of arbitration under s 27 of the Arbitration Act 1950.

### 8.16.5 Rent reviews

There are special problems with time provisions in the rent review clauses in leases, on which see part three of Bernstein and Reynolds.

### 8.16.6 Limitation

There is a statutory time limit of six years for claims under contracts under hand, and twelve if the contract is under seal: Limitation Act 1980 ss 5 and 8. Thus an expert's decision obtained after the limitation period will not be enforceable by court action: see Chapter 12.

## 8.17 Unclear expert clauses

### 8.17.1 Court can clarify an unclear clause

If an expert clause is unclear, it may have to be clarified by the court. This is ironic because the parties, having chosen expert determination, presumably wanted to avoid court proceedings. That the court has inherent discretionary jurisdiction to clarify the expert clause was stated in *Royal Trust International Ltd v Nordbanken* (1989) unreported, Chancery Division, 13 October:

... there may well be cases in which it is appropriate in the interests of the expert as well as the party [making the application to the court] that there should be an advance determination of law or construction which will form the basis of the expert's approach to his task.

### 8.17.2 Contractual rules of construction

The expert clause is a clause in a contract and it will therefore be subject to the same rules of interpretation as a contract. This means that express terms are interpreted according to what are known as the 'rules of construction' applied to contracts, and these contractual rules apply when attempts are made to imply terms which are needed to make sense of a contract. The same rules will also be applied to terms of reference, the procedure and the decision, all discussed in Chapter 11. Terms implied to make sense of a contract should be distinguished from terms implied by statute: for examples of terms implied by statute see 14.7.3 and

14.7.5. Relying on implied terms cannot be recommended, as it may take a great deal of time and money to obtain a satisfactory ruling from the court if the other party contests the implication.

### 8.17.3   Resolving ambiguities

The rules of construction applied to contracts are set out in *Chitty on Contracts*, Chapter 12, paras 808–883. Chitty states that the object of all construction is to discover the intentions of the parties and that the 'cardinal presumption' is that parties have intended what they have in fact said. The court will read the words of a contract by understanding the words used in their ordinary meaning, except where that would be absurd in the context. The contract should be read as a whole, rejecting those parts which are inconsistent. Rules have developed restricting the admissibility of evidence other than the written words of the contract. The rules do not prevent the use of extrinsic evidence in interpreting genuine ambiguities in the words of the contract. There is an example of the court interpreting express words to resolve an ambiguity in an expert clause in *Langham House Developments v Brompton Securities Ltd* (1980) 256 EG 719. A clause in a lease was silent about the status of the rent reviewer: all it said was that he was to be a surveyor. Was he to be an expert or an arbitrator? The judge decided that the surveyor was to be an expert, because the lease contained an underlease immediately preceding the rent review clause, and in the underlease the draftsman had used express words to specify the choice of procedure as arbitration—the disputed clause did not use any of those words —hence the surveyor was an expert.

### 8.17.4   Implied terms

Where the contract is silent on the consequences of an event which then occurs, the law of implied terms comes into play: see *Chitty on Contracts*, Chapter 13, paras 901–928. Four major principles stand out. The first is that a clause will be implied if it is necessary for the 'business efficacy' of the contract, and would have been accepted at once by both parties when making the contract: *The Moorcock* (1889) 14 PD 64 at 68. The second is that a term representing the obvious, necessary, but unexpressed intention of both parties will be implied: *Trollope & Colls Ltd v North West Metropolitan Regional Hospital Board* [1973] 1 WLR 601 at 609. The third is that a clause will not be implied merely because it would be reasonable: *Liverpool City Council v Irwin*

[1977] AC 239. The fourth is that the parties have an implied agreement to co-operate with each other: see, for example, *Panamena Europea Navigacion (Compania Limitada) v Frederick Leyland & Co Ltd (J Russell & Co)* [1947] AC 428 at 436. The extent of this last principle is uncertain.

### 8.17.5 *Importance of implied terms in expert determination*

Implied terms can be of great importance in expert cases, as can be seen from the remarks of Sir David Cairns in *Baber v Kenwood Manufacturing Co Ltd and Whinney Murray* [1978] 1 Lloyd's Rep 175 at 181, quoted at 13.5.4. Implied terms underpin the law of challenge to experts' decisions, because some basic terms are not spelled out: namely, that the parties would not accept a final decision intended to have binding effect when that decision was vitiated by dishonesty, partiality or mistake. Dishonesty and partiality are never mentioned in expert clauses as factors whose presence the parties agree would be sufficient to upset a decision: it is so obvious that it goes without saying, and is therefore an implied term. Mistake does appear occasionally in expert clauses as a circumstance in which the expert's decision would not be binding, but it is doubtful whether express words to that effect alter the principle implied by the court: see 13.11.

### 8.17.6 *Would the courts imply the terms in 8.4–8.16?*

Can the law of implied terms be used to imply any other of the elements of an expert clause set out earlier in this chapter? Very few of those elements would pass any of the tests.

### 8.17.7 *Construction summonses*

Recent decisions of the court (see 13.6 and 13.9) have made it very much more difficult to raise construction issues after the decision. Before the reference has got under way, the most likely procedure will be the construction summons. An application can be made to the court to obtain a ruling by issuing an originating summons under RSC Ord 7, seeking a declaration in the terms of the meaning desired.

# Chapter 9

# Qualifications of an Expert

## 9.1 Summary

This chapter explains:
(1) that the identity and qualifications of an expert are established by the parties, usually in the expert clause, and that an expert need not be an individual (9.2);
(2) the practice of referring disputes to a named individual, firm or company (9.3);
(3) the same practice where the test is the position held by an individual, firm or company (9.4);
(4) the practice of referring disputes to members of a particular profession (9.5);
(5) the effect of stipulating criteria for an expert's eligibility (9.6);
(6) the effect of a requirement that an expert be independent (9.7);
(7) the practice relating to umpires (9.8).

## 9.2 Person, firm or company?

### 9.2.1 A firm or company can act as expert

An expert need not be an individual person. A firm, such as a firm of accountants that has been appointed auditors to a company, can be an expert: see 3.4. Even a company can be an expert. It is usual, for instance, in trust deeds used in the capital markets to provide that disputes about remuneration of the trustee are to be resolved by a merchant bank acting as an expert: see 5.5.

### 9.2.2 Appointment of a firm or company more common in commercial application

Clauses which provide for the expert to be a firm or company are usually found in commercial applications of the type considered in Chapters 2–5. Technical questions of the type considered in Chapter 7 could be determined by a firm or company, but the practice is rare. Rarer still is the resolution of general disputes under a contract (discussed in 6.9) by a non-individual.

### 9.2.3 Expert determination need not be a personal process

The courts do not appear to have been troubled by the notion of an issue being determined by an expert other than an individual. This may demonstrate one of the essential features of expert determination, namely that it need not be a personal process. It certainly underlines the court's policy of giving effect to the contract between the parties, rather than seeking to establish general rules about who is qualified to act as an expert.

### 9.2.4 Expert clause must designate the expert

It is therefore essential to examine the expert clause which should state who the expert is to be, whether:
(1) a named individual (see 9.3); or
(2) a named firm or company (see 9.3); or
(3) the individual, firm or company holding a particular position (see 9.4); or
(4) a member of a particular profession or a holder of a particular academic or professional qualification (see 9.5); and whether
(5) there are any special criteria for the expert's suitability (see 9.6).

Each of these is examined in the sections which follow.


### 9.3 A named individual, firm or company

#### 9.3.1 A named individual may not be available when needed

Referring issues to a named individual is not advised unless a dispute has already arisen, because some time may pass after the making of the original contract containing the reference to the specifically named individual, and by the time a dispute arises that individual may have died, retired, become ill, have a conflict of interest or be otherwise unavailable or unsuitable.

### 9.3.2 *Similarly with a firm or company*

Referring issues to a named firm or company can run into similar problems but, again, it is appropriate when a dispute has already arisen: see 8.2.4.

### 9.3.3 *Potential deadlock*

Naming specific experts in the expert clause may allow an awkward party to create insoluble deadlock: see 10.3.3.

## 9.4 An individual, firm or company holding a particular position

### 9.4.1 *Share valuation and auditors' firms*

Referring issues to the firm holding a particular position is especially popular in share valuation and other functions entrusted to the firm of auditors for the time being of the company in question.

### 9.4.2 *Not found with individuals or companies*

There is no reason why something similar should not happen with individuals or companies, but there are no recorded instances.

## 9.5 A member of a particular profession or a holder of a particular academic or professional qualification

### 9.5.1 *Professional qualifications preferred*

Referring issues to a member of a particular profession has become more and more prevalent in parallel with the growth of the importance of the professions. As has already been seen in the earlier chapters, the professions most often specified are surveyors, accountants, actuaries and engineers. The qualification may be membership of a particular professional body or the holding of a particular academic degree or professional certificate. Professional qualifications are stipulated much more commonly than academic degrees.

### 9.5.2 *No qualifications necessary unless expert clause says so*

However, unless the expert clause says so or it is agreed by the parties before the appointment is made, the expert need have no particular qualifications at all. As so often is the case, it all depends on the wording of the expert clause. Experts are frequently appointed by professional bodies acting as appointing authorities. For a discussion of the potential liability of appointing authorities for appointing unqualified experts, see 9.6.

### 9.6 Criteria for an expert's suitability

#### 9.6.1 Need to be specific

The expert clause may lay down criteria for the expert's suitability. Where this is a matter of education and experience, it is best to specify an academic degree, professional certificate or membership of a professional body. A clause which says no more than that the expert is to be 'suitably qualified' can provide material for a wasteful argument if a dispute arises subsequently.

#### 9.6.2 Liability of appointing authority

Some expert clauses seek to make the appointing authority (or its president) responsible for ensuring the expert has suitable qualifications. A clause of this type could be relied on in an action against an appointing authority for failing to appoint a suitably qualified person. The argument would run that the appointing authority would have seen the clause (as they always ask to do) before making the appointment, would have taken a fee for making the appointment, that the arrangement was therefore a contract incorporating the clause about suitability, and that an aggrieved party could sue for breach of that term of the contract.

#### 9.6.3 An implied term?

Where there is no clause of this type, the aggrieved party would have to argue that there was an implied term (see 8.17.4) in the appointment contract that the authority would appoint a suitably qualified person. An appointing authority could seek to exclude the implied term by express words, but that would not be an attractive course: appointing authorities have reputations to keep.

#### 9.6.4 Tortious liability

Where there is no fee charged by the appointing authority for the appointment there would be no 'consideration' and therefore no contract. The tortious liability of the appointing authority under *Hedley Byrne & Co Ltd v Heller & Partners Ltd* [1964] AC 465 would have to be investigated, with the probable result that the authority would be found to have owed a duty of care: see 14.11.

## 9.7 Independence

### 9.7.1 Meaning

Independence is clearly a desirable quality in an expert: no one would be against it. But what does 'independence' mean? It does not mean that an expert's decision would be disallowed on the ground of conflict of interest: actual partiality would have to be shown. See further 10.8 on conflicts of interest and 13.3.2 on partiality.

### 9.7.2 Drafting traditions

. Draftsmen often use the word 'independent', as in phrases like 'an independent valuer' or 'an independent accountant': the latter is used in the precedents in Appendix A. Sometimes this wording seems to have been intended to draw a distinction between expert determination and arbitration, as in the clause in the lease which was disputed in *North Eastern Cooperative Society Ltd v Newcastle Upon Tyne City Council* [1987] 1 EGLR 142, where the parties were supposed to agree on 'an independent surveyor', and if they could not agree, the RICS was to appoint an arbitrator. But other leases contain wording which says that the *arbitrator* must be 'an independent surveyor': so the wording of each clause will have to be considered to see whether the word 'independent' carries any particular message about the status of the referee.

## 9.8 Umpires

### 9.8.1 Nineteenth century procedure

Some expert clauses have referred the issue not just to one expert but to two experts and an umpire. From the cases, this seems to have been common practice in the nineteenth century: see for instance *Re Carus-Wilson & Greene* (1886) 18 QBD 7, where there were two valuers and an umpire to value timber in a land sale. A typical procedure is that each party appoints a valuer; the two party-appointed valuers should meet and try to agree the valuation, and, if they are unable to agree, the matter is referred to an umpire appointed by the valuers. This procedure is open to sabotage by an awkward party, but the law will now help: see 10.3.3.

### 9.8.2 Similar modern practice

Modern practice has moved away from official reference to two experts and an umpire so described, but the procedures are often quite similar in practice. For instance, in *Jones v Sherwood Computer Services plc* [1991] NPC 60, the sale and purchase agreement said that a sales statement prepared by the purchasers was to be reviewed by the vendors' and the purchasers' accountants. Those accountants were to seek to approve the statement or agree on an adjusted version, and only if they could not agree would the matter then be referred to an expert. The agreement also said that all the accountants concerned were acting as experts.

### 9.8.3 Umpires both experts and arbitrators

The umpire procedure has often been relied on as an argument for a reference being an arbitration rather than an instance of expert determination (or, in the older cases, a 'valuation') but the courts have not seen the umpire procedure as an important factor, and the involvement of an umpire does not turn a reference to an expert into an arbitration. This has been recently reaffirmed in *Safeway Food Stores Ltd v Banderway Ltd* (1983) 267 EG 850, where the judge said that the word 'umpire' was quite neutral and did not cast any light on the nature of the reference.

# Chapter 10

# Appointing an Expert

## 10.1 Summary

This chapter:
(1) describes how an expert is appointed, either by the parties or by a professional body (10.2);
(2) explains the problems created by the absence of effective appointment machinery independent of the parties (10.3);
(3) shows how an appointment may be invalid (10.4);
(4) provides a list of appointing authorities with figures for some of their rates of appointments (10.5);
(5) outlines procedures for making an application to an appointing authority (10.6);
(6) shows that the court will not help parties obstruct appointments (10.7);
(7) considers the difficulties that can arise from perceived conflicts of interest (10.8).

## 10.2 Appointment by the parties

### 10.2.1 Auditors and share valuation

Where the expert clause establishes the identity of the expert conclusively, it will not be necessary to provide for the selection and appointment of the expert. However, these cases will be rare, and probably the only exception encountered with any frequency will be the appointment of a company's auditors to value its shares.

### 10.2.2 All other cases

Many expert clauses provide that the parties should, in the first instance, try to agree on the expert to whom the issue will be referred. This method of appointment has the merits of being quick and cheap. But without the sanction of a clause dealing with appointment where the parties cannot agree, it is no use at all where one party makes a policy decision to reject every nominee proposed by the other party. The parties therefore need to have agreed that, where they cannot agree on the identity of an expert, the appointment may be made by a third party.

### 10.2.3 Appointing authorities

A well-drafted clause will state that, if the parties cannot agree on who is to be the expert, a specified body will make the appointment on the application of either party. That body, almost always a professional association, then becomes known as 'the appointing authority'. For a precedent, see Appendix A 1.1. The function of the appointing authority is simply to appoint the expert: they do not supervise the subsequent conduct of the reference, as is the case for some arbitrations which are supervised by arbitration bodies such as the International Chamber of Commerce or the London Court of International Arbitration.

## 10.3 Absence of effective appointment machinery

### 10.3.1 The court cannot appoint experts

Where an appointment provision is necessary, but the clause does not include one, there can be difficulties. Without the appointing authority, there is no means by which an expert can be appointed. The court does not have the power to appoint experts in private references: its power to appoint arbitrators arises under ss 7 and 10 of the Arbitration Act 1950: there is no similar statutory provision for experts, and no inherent power.

### 10.3.2 Particular difficulty with umpire procedure

There used to be a particular difficulty in clauses providing for the appointment of valuers by each party who would then refer the matter to an umpire: see 9.8.1. (The cases all concern referees known as 'valuers', but the same difficulty could arise with experts if the umpire procedure were used for experts, which modern practice has made rare: see 9.8.2.) Draftsmen found an answer by providing that, if either party neglected to appoint a valuer, the valuation provided by the other party's valuer would be binding. But, where the clause did not contain that useful provision, an awkward party ran no risk in simply refusing to appoint a valuer, with the result that the reference could not go ahead and there was no way of obtaining a valuation.

### 10.3.3   Sudbrook v Eggleton *breaks the deadlock*

For many years the court refused to help, but the House of Lords overturned the old authorities in *Sudbrook Trading Estate Ltd v Eggleton* [1983] AC 444: the line of precedent went back to *Milnes v Gery* (1807) 14 Ves Jun 399 at 400. In *Sudbrook* the lessors had refused to appoint their valuer to discuss and seek to agree the value of the reversions with a valuer appointed by the lessees; under the lease the valuers appointed were to refer the matter to an umpire. The result was that the procedure was deadlocked and no umpire could be appointed, because that could be achieved only by an act of the two valuers after they had both been appointed. The House of Lords broke the deadlock by ordering an inquiry to be conducted by the court into the value of the reversions: it did not order the lessors to appoint a valuer. The court cannot supply the valuation if it is an essential element of the contract that the valuation be conducted by a named individual: *Sudbrook* p 483–4.

### 10.3.4   *Other types of deadlock*

It is to be hoped that this can be applied to other similar situations of deadlock. Badly drafted clauses sometimes encountered say that the expert must be acceptable to both parties, or that he is to be appointed by some person or institution acceptable to both parties. An awkward party could block the procedure by declaring unacceptable every expert or appointing individual or authority put forward by the other party.

### 10.4   Validity of appointment

### 10.4.1   *What does the validity depend on?*

Whether an appointment is valid depends on the interpretation of the agreement providing that the appointment is to be made, correspondence between the parties about the appointment, and the acts of an appointing authority.

### 10.4.2   *Conditional agreements*

The effects of correspondence between the parties were considered in *Darlington Borough Council v Waring & Gillow (Holdings) Ltd* [1988] 2 EGLR 159. In that case there had been a failure to make an application to appoint an independent surveyor within the time limit in the lease. The parties then wrote letters to each other about a proposed appointment of a surveyor to review the rent. Both parties marked their letters with a variety of combinations of expressions like 'without prejudice', 'subject to contract', and 'subject to approval by . . .'. The court held that the effect of these conditions was that no agreement to appoint the expert had taken place, and the whole procedure was invalid.

### 10.4.3 Appointor cannot appoint himself

Unsurprisingly, the court has held that a person charged with making an appointment cannot validly appoint himself as the expert: *Jones (M) v Jones (R R)* [1971] 1 WLR 840.

## 10.5 Appointing authorities

### 10.5.1 Advantages of appointing authorities

The provision in the expert clause of a person or institution to make the appointment where the parties cannot agree avoids the risk of deadlock and should also help to ensure that a suitable person is appointed.

### 10.5.2 Is the appointing authority willing to act?

Care should be taken to ensure that the person or institution designated by the expert clause to take on this role is willing to do so. There are some precedents of expert clauses in circulation naming certain bodies as appointing authorities which do not undertake that function. If the person or institution is not willing, the clause may be ineffective, because the contract will not be binding on that person or institution and the court will not make the appointment: see 10.3.1.

### 10.5.3 List of appointing authorities

The following institutions state that they act as appointing authorities. They share the characteristic of being established recognised professional bodies:
- The Association of Consulting Engineers;
- The Chartered Institute of Arbitrators;
- The Chartered Institute of Management Accountants;
- The Chartered Institute of Patent Agents;
- The Incorporated Society of Valuers and Auctioneers;
- The Institute of Actuaries;

- The Institute of Chartered Accountants in England and Wales;
- The Institute of Petroleum;
- The Law Society of England and Wales;
- The Royal Institute of British Architects;
- The Royal Institution of Chartered Surveyors.

(1) The RICS appointed 11,500 surveyors in 1989 and 14,550 in 1990, either as experts or arbitrators: no separate statistics are available, but the RICS believes that 55 per cent were experts and 45 per cent were arbitrators.

(2) The ISVA appoint about 300 surveyors per year, with about 100 of those being experts, and about 200 being arbitrators.

(3) The ICAEW appointed 70 accountants in 1990; only 2 or 3 were arbitrators, the rest were experts.

(4) The Law Society makes an average of 50–60 appointments each year, of which only 2 or 3 are experts, the remainder being arbitrators.

(5) The number of experts appointed by the other bodies is very small.

(6) For the addresses and telephone numbers of these bodies see Appendix F.

### 10.5.4 Appointment by a president

In many cases the clause provides that the appointment is to be by the president (for the time being) of the body concerned. This will cause difficulty if the institution does not appoint a president. It is probably unnecessary to specify the president, as the relevant institution's procedures will be similar even if the president is not specified. The Law Society has published their procedure: where the president of the Law Society is to make an appointment, his staff draw up a short list and the president places the names in the order of his preference: see Appendix B.

### 10.6 Application to the appointing authority

#### 10.6.1 By letter

With most of these bodies an application by letter will be sufficient, but the letter should take care to set out the request in a convenient way. The letter should specify the parties, the contract, the expert clause and the issue to be resolved, at the very least, and further details may be useful.

## 10.6.2    Application forms and fees

No doubt because of the large volume of applications in connection with rent reviews, the RICS and the ISVA have established more formal procedures. Both bodies publish application
forms recommended for use when applying to them for the
appointment of experts or arbitrators: copies of the forms are
reproduced in Appendices G and H. The Law Society has also
published its requested procedure: see [1986] *Law Society's
Gazette* 2542, reprinted in Appendix B. It is important that applicants follow the procedure of applying on prescribed forms.
Those who just write a letter have found their informal requests
ignored completely or at least not dealt with for some time. There
is usually a fee to be paid, in 1991 generally around the £100 mark
plus VAT. Flat fees used to be the rule, but since 1 January 1991
the Law Society has introduced a sliding scale of up to £1,000: see
Appendix B. The ISVA charge no fee.

## 10.6.3    Effect of formal procedures

In *Staines Warehousing Co Ltd v Montagu Executor & Trustee
Ltd* [1987] 2 EGLR 130 the court held that where a lease provides
that an application to appoint a surveyor is to be made to a
specified appointing body like the RICS, the application had to
follow the procedures laid down by that appointing body. The
RICS guidance notes said that an application could be made by
letter, although it would not be processed until the official form
had been completed and the fee paid.

## 10.7    Attempts to prevent appointments

### 10.7.1    Can an appointment be prevented?

Will the court prevent an appointing authority from making an
appointment because one of the parties objects to the reference
proceeding? This question was raised in *United Cooperatives Ltd
v Sun Alliance & London Assurance Co Ltd* [1987] 1 EGLR 126.
Tenants tried to injunct the president of the RICS from appointing an independent surveyor to act as an expert in a rent review.
They said the appointment would be premature because they
were contemplating proceedings for rectification of the lease and
the expert could not determine the rent until after those proceedings: and there were also arguments about the interpretation of
notice periods relating to the rent review.

*10.7.2    The court refused to grant an injunction*

The president of the RICS at the time filed evidence about his practice for dealing with the very large number of applications for appointments of rent review experts and arbitrators (7,664 in 1985: but see 10.5.3 above – 14,550 in 1990). The RICS check each lease to make sure there is a power of appointment; other than that, the president did not consider it his function to determine any legal questions which might arise in the course of a rent review. The judge refused to grant an injunction, and said it was for the valuer to decide whether to proceed or not, and that the president of the RICS owed no duty to the parties not to make an appointment. It is likely that the court would take a similar attitude to attempts to stop appointments by other bodies.

## 10.8    Conflicts of interest

*10.8.1    Other commercial relationships*

Appointing authorities sometimes get drawn into arguments about whether members of certain professional firms could be independent in a dispute because of their firm's relationship with one of the parties. This delays the appointment and adds to the work of the appointing authority.

*10.8.2    RICS policy statement*

The RICS has issued a 'policy statement on alleged conflicts of interest'. This states that the result of objections has sometimes been an attempt to exclude every specialist in a given field. The statement says that the president of the RICS will give careful weight to objections, but then reach his own decision. The RICS appointment procedures include asking potential appointees to disclose matters which would compromise independence.

*10.8.3    Accountancy firms*

Accountants have similar though less well-publicised problems. Clauses often say that the accountant appointed as an expert must be a partner in an 'international' firm, which has been interpreted to mean one of what used to be the 'big eight' firms. Mergers between these firms have had the effect of reducing the number of accountants who do not have a conflict of interest, simply because there are fewer firms. Also, different departments of the chief accountancy firms often have client relationships with the other party to the dispute, as many clients prefer not to give all their work to one firm. The result can be that all the experts who would otherwise be suitable are 'conflicted out', in today's inelegant but pithy expression. The ICAEW resolve the problem by choosing an expert from amongst the top 20–30 firms, rather than those who used to be called the 'big eight'.

### 10.8.4 Insufficient to justify a challenge

Conflicts of interest giving rise to concerns about lack of independence are insufficient to justify a challenge to an expert's decision: see 13.3.2.

# Chapter 11

# Procedure for the reference

## 11.1  Summary

This chapter examines the progress in a reference after the expert has been appointed, and explains:
(1) that there is no set procedure outside the contract (11.2);
(2) that there may be nothing in the contract about the procedure (11.3);
(3) terms of reference (11.4);
(4) procedural directions (11.5);
(5) conduct of the investigation (11.6);
(6) the form of the decision (11.7);
(7) that there are no published procedures for specific applications except the RICS guidance notes (11.8).

This chapter should be read in conjunction with the precedents in Appendix A.

## 11.2  No set procedure except the contract

### 11.2.1  Expert clause: the only decisive document

The law lays down no set procedure for the manner in which an expert should conduct a reference. Expert determination is not a type of legal proceeding like litigation, which has a formal and highly regulated structure, nor does it have machinery for its supervision by judges as does arbitration. The expert clause in the parties' contract will be the only document likely to have a decisive effect, and then only if it lays down the procedure in detail, which many do not do. It might help to do so in special or novel applications.

### 11.2.2  The court may help

The court has jurisdiction to decide issues of the construction of expert clauses both before and probably during a reference (see 8.17.1) but not afterwards, except, possibly, with the consent of both parties (see 13.9). The court will decide those issues on the hearing of a construction summons, and may also grant an injunction to stop a reference being conducted on the wrong basis. The issues are limited to interpretation of the words of the expert clause or other relevant parts of the original contract, or the interpretation of terms of reference or other agreed procedure. Questions of fairness of the procedure will be decided by interpreting the contract rather than by reference to an external standard. Thus if an expert and the parties are faced with an ambiguous or impossible procedure laid down by contract, the court may be able to help them work out what they are supposed to do. However, the words of the governing document will have more significance than the more recent correspondence or terms of reference, if any: see *Nikko Hotels (UK) Ltd v MEPC Ltd* 28 EG 86 at 99.

### 11.2.3 Procedure set out in expert clauses

For a discussion of the words about procedure found in expert clauses, see 8.15. They may provide:
  (1) no guidance at all, or
  (2) the right to make submissions, or even
  (3) full details of the procedure with time limits.

## 11.3 Where no procedure is laid down in the contract

### 11.3.1 General

Where the contract does not lay down a procedure, the expert will have to do so. He may receive suggestions from the parties on which they may agree and which he can adopt. Suggestions for procedure which have evolved in practice and are commonly accepted are considered in 11.5.

### 11.3.2 Settled between expert and parties

Procedure is usually discussed between the expert and the parties. This may be achieved by correspondence, but a meeting may be necessary, and is almost always desirable. If the parties agree on a procedure and the expert does not, the parties should appoint another expert. If one of the parties agrees with the expert and the other does not, that other party may, depending on the circumstances, be in breach of the contract to refer the matter to an expert which carries with it an obligation to follow directions issued by the expert: see the example at 11.5.3.

## 11.4    Terms of reference

### 11.4.1    Ensuring the right basis

Whatever procedure is followed must ensure that:
(1) the expert has the basic information about the issue he is to decide and who he is to decide it between;
(2) the expert has a copy of the contract with the expert clause.

These points should present no difficulty, particularly if the expert has been appointed by an appointing authority. They are sometimes called 'terms of reference'. Terms of reference can also describe the documents leading up to the expert's investigation of the issue. These could be, for example:
(1) the original contract;
(2) the letter of appointment; and
(3) a summary of the issues to be determined.

### 11.4.2    Other matters can be covered

Terms of reference that go beyond these matters will result from discussions between the parties, and probably the expert as well, where it is convenient to have terms of reference separate from procedural directions. In those cases the parties and the expert should take the opportunity of securing a precise definition of the issue the expert is to decide. That definition will have to keep the issue within the framework of the parties' original contract, but precision within that framework will save costs and uncertainty. They should also address the question of the expert's fees and expenses. The expert clause may say how the fees and expenses are to be apportioned: if not, this must be decided. The rate or amount of the fee can be settled at this stage. Any other matters not covered in the expert clause can also be dealt with in terms of reference.

## 11.5    Procedural directions

### 11.5.1    Representations

Even though some expert clauses do not specifically reserve the right for the parties to make submissions or representations to the expert (see 8.15), it is unlikely that this right will be lost through its omission, because the expert will usually want to receive submissions or representations of some kind to help him understand the issue he has to determine. The expert will in most cases want each party to send him a written submission accompanied by copies of the documents referred to or relied on in the submission. It is usual and desirable to provide that each party is to be sent a copy of the other party's submission. A case where the claim was set out in one letter agreed by both parties and a later, unilateral, submission was not copied to the other party is discussed in 13.13.2. Views differ as to whether submissions should be exchanged simultaneously or whether one party's submission should follow the other's. In some cases the parties may wish to keep their respective submissions confidential from each other, and there is nothing inherently objectionable in that, provided it is clearly agreed between the parties and the expert.

### 11.5.2   Timing

Procedural directions should include provision for the publication of the expert's decision, and whether it should give reasons; and it is obviously desirable to set a timetable for submissions and a decision. However, difficulties may arise if a strict time limit is set for the publication of the decision, and the decision is published after it has expired: it may suit one of the parties to refuse to accept it on that ground. The expert does, in any case, have a statutory obligation to deliver a timely decision: see 14.7.3.

### 11.5.3   Inspections

The expert may need to do more than receive submissions, and directions should be given about the arrangements for physical inspections, site visits and the like. Where these arrangements need the co-operation of one or other of the parties, the court will make an order if necessary to enforce that co-operation. In *Smith v Peters* (1875) LR 20 Eq 511, there was an agreement for the sale of fixtures and fittings of a public house at a valuation by a person named by both parties. The vendor refused to let that person into the public house. The court made a mandatory order compelling the vendor to allow the person to enter so that the valuation could proceed. Giving judgment, Sir George Jessel MR said that there was no limit to the practice of the court with regard to interlocutory applications ancillary to the administration of justice.

## 11.5.4 Legal advice

Consideration should be given as to whether the expert will need outside assistance such as legal advice in order to complete his work. The expert will seek the parties' agreement to the principle and the cost of obtaining that outside assistance. For an instance where one of the parties did object to the principle, see *Chelsea Man plc v Vivat Holdings plc* (1989) unreported, Court of Appeal, 24 August discussed at 13.8.2: and for two examples of how an expert dealt with points of law, see 13.8.3. An expert cannot get this sort of help from the court, as can an arbitrator: see 16.3.4.

## 11.5.5 Litigation-type procedures

The remaining question is the extent to which the expert and the parties allow the reference to resemble arbitration (or even litigation). This will depend on the nature of the dispute and the extent of the part played by lawyers in the proceedings, but, for the reasons set out below, lawyers will serve their clients' interests better if they refrain from imposing too many legal formalities on the procedure. For instance, should the parties be ordered to disclose documents on a wide-ranging basis similar to the 'discovery' procedures of the court? Discovery obliges each party to disclose to the other *all* documents relevant to the issues, except those containing legal advice on those issues. Should the parties be allowed to examine and cross-examine witnesses? Should they be allowed to conduct a formal hearing? All of these features have appeared in expert determinations. Their intrinsic value will usually be outweighed by the extra cost and time taken as well as the danger of the procedure being turned into an arbitration: see 15.7. As is explained in the next section, informal arrangements may be preferable.

## 11.6 Conduct of the investigation

### 11.6.1 Informality preferred

With what degree of formality should the investigation be conducted? The anecdotal evidence is that parties often want informal, non-legalistic meetings where the expert can hear what the parties' non-legal representatives have to say, without any lawyers being present. Meetings of this type are not 'hearings' in the litigation sense. These meetings may include an element of mediation. The expert will want to make sure he understands both points of view, and in doing so, he may decide that he should try to persuade one or both of the parties about the other's position. He will also wish to find the common ground shared by the parties and build on it. The expert is not precluded from taking this role unless the parties agree to prohibit him from doing so.

### 11.6.2 Avoid suggestions of impartiality

In these discussions the prudent expert will avoid conduct which might be thought to cast doubt on his partiality. In the finance leasing case *Midland Montagu Leasing (UK) Ltd v Tyne & Wear Passenger Transport Executive and Ernst & Whinney* (1990) unreported, Chancery Division, 23 February an expert had discussions with both parties about the form of his certificate. He also attended a meeting at which the lessors and their solicitors discussed tactics for dealing with the lessees. The court said that the expert should have remained aloof from the tactical discussions. However, that did not invalidate the expert's decision, and there was nothing wrong in the expert meeting both of the parties to discuss his certificate. The expert refused to do what the lessors wanted him to do, namely to rewrite his certificate in a way which he thought would make the certificate conclusive against the lessees' interests. Ironically, the court found the certificate conclusive anyway: see 13.7.7.

### 11.6.3 Expert pursuing his own investigations

An expert can pursue his own investigations into the issue he has to decide, and traditionally that is one of the functions which differentiates his role from that of an arbitrator: 15.6.3. He does not, however, have to pursue his own investigations if the parties have provided him with sufficient evidence: 14.8. There is nothing to stop the parties specifically preventing the expert from pursuing his own investigations and limiting his consideration of evidence to the material submitted by the parties; this can be attended to at this stage, if it has not been already provided for in the expert clause: see 8.15.8.

### 11.6.4 Disclosure of documents

The parties will probably wish to provide the expert with documents supporting their respective cases. Difficulties can arise if one party refuses to disclose a document which the other party wishes the expert to see. Unless there is a specific provision about this in the expert clause (see 8.15.10), the expert will have less authority to impose disclosure on an unwilling party: but he can draw adverse inferences from the failure to disclose. General disclosure directions, such as those under discovery procedures of the court (see 11.5.5) are not likely to be either welcome or appropriate.

### 11.6.5 Defamation

Can an expert or the parties be sued for defamation for remarks made in the course of a reference? There is no direct authority. References to experts are likely to be seen as occasions of what is known as 'qualified privilege', where a plaintiff can succeed in a defamation action only if he can prove malice on the part of the defendant. The privilege would be 'absolute', which means that nothing, including evidence of malice, could rebut it, if the court found that the reference to the expert closely resembled judicial proceedings. This should not be used as an excuse for making references more legalistic.

## 11.7  The decision

### 11.7.1  Form of the decision

The decision, which is usually in the form of a letter from the expert, should set out:

- the name of the expert;
- the names of the parties;
- the issue they asked the expert to determine;
- the relevant contract and expert clause;
- the manner by which the expert was appointed;
- the terms of reference;
- the procedural directions;
- compliance (or otherwise) by the parties with those directions;
- the decision itself (see 11.7.2);
- the fees and expenses;
  and, whatever its form, the decision should be signed and dated.

### 11.7.2  Reasons

The decision itself is likely to be a brief answer to the question put: for a one-line example see the decision in *Jones v Sherwood Computer Services plc* [1991] NPC 60, quoted at 13.6.4. The provision of reasons for decisions has become unpopular because reasons give more ammunition for challenge and negligence claims: see 14.7.7. If the expert is obliged by earlier agreement to give reasons, then he must do so: if he has not agreed beforehand to give reasons, he cannot be compelled to do so: see 13.7.8. Apart from the decision on the question put and any reasons, the decision should also deal with interest and costs, to the extent that these matters are within the expert's jurisdiction: see 8.10–8.13.

## 11.8   Procedures for specific applications

### 11.8.1   Rent reviews

Part four of the RICS guidance notes (published in Bernstein and Reynolds), deals with recommended procedures for the independent expert conducting a rent review. The notes recommend that the expert call a preliminary meeting to establish the terms of his appointment and the procedure for the reference, and set out a number of matters specific to rent review as well as the more general principles.

### 11.8.2   Other applications

There are no published guides for other applications. Appendix A contains precedents which can be adapted to suit the occasion.

Chapter 12

# Enforcing the Decision

## 12.1 Summary

This chapter explains whether, and if so how, an expert's decision may be enforced, and explains
(1) the nature of enforcement procedures (12.2);
(2) the use of court action to enforce experts' decisions (12.3);
(3) the use of the threat of insolvency (12.4);
(4) enforcement by the use of set-off (12.5);
(5) difficulties with enforcement abroad (12.6); and
(6) time limitation on enforcement (12.7).

## 12.2 Enforcement procedures

### 12.2.1 Securing compliance with an expert's decision

'Enforcement' means sanctions for non-compliance, of which a range are available against those who disobey judgments and orders of the court. An example of enforcement is 'execution', which means seizure and removal of the defendant's goods to the value of the unsatisfied judgment plus interest and costs. The threat of enforcement is often sufficient to secure payment.

### 12.2.2 An expert's decision cannot be enforced as an arbitration award

A decision of an expert is not the result of a judicial examination of a dispute, and no statute has been enacted providing enforcement machinery. An arbitration award can be enforced by application to the court under s 26 of the Arbitration Act 1950, which allows enforcement of the award in the same way as if it were a court judgment. Can an expert's decision be enforced under s 26 as an arbitration award? There is no direct authority on this point, although the differences between arbitration and expert determination should be sufficient to ensure that enforcement of experts' decisions under the section would not be permitted. At first sight *A Cameron Ltd v John Mowlem & Co Ltd* (1990) 52 BLR 24 provides guidance, but the case was decided on rather different grounds. The Court of Appeal considered whether an adjudicator's decision in a construction contract (see 6.8.5) was enforceable as an arbitration award, and decided that it was not, but their judgment was based on the *interim* nature of the adjudicator's decision pending arbitration to which the decision would be subject, and not on any of the usual characteristics of experts' decisions: the interim nature of adjudicators' decisions is itself untypical of experts' decisions.

### 12.2.3 Insolvency

The threat of insolvency can, however, be made without court proceedings as a necessary preliminary: see 12.4.

### 12.2.4 Leases

Leases contain their own procedures for defaulting tenants who do not pay the increased rental determined by an expert.

## 12.3 Court action

### 12.3.1 Plaintiff will seek summary judgment

Unless the threat of insolvency can be successfully used (12.4), court action will be necessary. Refusal by a party to comply with the decision is a breach of contract — so the plaintiff will plead the contractual background, the determination by the expert and the default. The plaintiff will probably wish to seek summary judgment under RSC Ord 14: by this procedure, he will be able to oblige the defendant to put in affidavit evidence of his defence (if there is one) to the claim. The court action will of course give the defendant the opportunity to challenge the decision: Chapter 13 sets out the grounds on which challenge is allowed.

### 12.3.2 Likely orders made

If the plaintiff is successful in the RSC Ord 14 proceedings, the court will give judgment in his favour with costs. This will be a final judgment, but subject to the defendant's right to appeal. If the defendant is successful in the RSC Ord 14 proceedings, the court may make various orders, including allowing the defendant to defend the claim, which means that the plaintiff's next opportunity to obtain judgment against the defendant will not arise before the end of a full trial. This 'leave to defend', as it is called, may have conditions attached to it, such as the defendant paying into court part or all of the amount claimed.

## 12.4 Insolvency

### 12.4.1 Demands

If the party obliged to make a payment as the result of an expert's decision does not do so, he may, if he is an individual, be served with a statutory demand under s 268 of the Insolvency Act 1986; or, if the defaulting party is a company, it may be served with a written demand under s 123 of the Insolvency Act 1986. The effect of both these procedures is that the defaulting party has 21 days in which to make the payment, following which the party making the demand can present a bankruptcy petition against an individual or a winding-up petition against a company.

### 12.4.2 An effective means of enforcement

If there is a defence to liability for the amount determined, the party seeking the bankruptcy or winding-up order may be ordered to pay the costs of the insolvency proceedings. If there is no defence however, this may be a very effective means of enforcement.

## 12.5 Set-off

### 12.5.1 Enforcement without court action

If the potential plaintiff has other dealings with the potential defendant, these may give him the opportunity to exercise rights of set-off. In other words, the potential plaintiff may withhold payment of money which is due to the potential defendant, as an alternative way of obtaining the benefit of the expert's decision. This may provide a means of enforcement without immediate court action.

### 12.5.2 Court action may result

This kind of self-help may provoke an action from the other party to recover the payment that has been withheld: or, if the other party is a defendant in proceedings with the same plaintiff, withholding the payment may provoke a counterclaim.

## 12.6 Difficulties with enforcement abroad

### 12.6.1 Reciprocal enforcement of judgments and arbitration awards

Court judgments and arbitration awards may be enforced in countries other than England under various treaties. For court judgments there is, for the European Community, the 1968 Brussels Convention, made part of English law by the Civil Jurisdiction and Judgments Act 1982, and reciprocal enforcement treaties with various other countries under the Administration of Justice Act 1920 and the Foreign Judgments (Reciprocal Enforcement) Act 1933. For arbitrations there is the 1958 New York Convention, incorporated as part of English law by the Arbitration Act 1975.

### 12.6.2 No such machinery for experts' decisions

Decisions by experts cannot be enforced abroad in this way. It will be necessary either to take court action in England to turn the decision into a judgment which may then be enforced abroad through a treaty, or to take court action in the country where enforcement is desired. It may be an advantage for the expert's decision of which enforcement is sought to be accompanied by reasons, because the foreign court is likely to be more sympathetic to enforcing it in that form.

### 12.6.3 Expert determination not advised for international contracts

Careful consideration should be given before using the expert procedure in a contract where enforcement of the decision abroad might be necessary. Particular attention should be paid to the means of enforcement (if any) in the other country and to the likely attitude of the foreign court. It is for these reasons that expert determination is not recommended in international contracts.

## 12.7 Limitation

### 12.7.1 General six-year period

The time limit for enforcing an expert's decision is the same as that for enforcing other contracts, six years if the contract to refer to the expert is under hand, twelve in the unlikely case of its being under seal: s 5 and s 8 of the Limitation Act 1980. Time runs from the date of the breach, which will usually be the date of non-compliance with the decision.

### 12.7.2  Section 7 of the Limitation Act 1980

An expert's decision is probably not an 'award' within s 7 of the Limitation Act 1980, on the assumption that an award would be issued by an arbitrator and not an expert: see further 12.2.2.

# Chapter 13

# Challenging the Decision

## 13.1  Summary

This chapter looks at the limited right of challenge to the validity of an expert's decision, and explains:

    (1) that it is the parties to a contract who get involved in various kinds of court proceedings where the validity of the decision is challenged, and not the expert (13.2);

    (2) the grounds for challenge (13.3);

    (3) the earlier history of the law of mistake in expert determination (13.4);

    (4) more recent developments (13.5);

    (5) the current position (13.6);

    (6) speaking and non-speaking decisions (13.7);

    (7) points of law (13.8);

    (8) construction of documents (13.9);

    (9) various other aspects of mistake (13.10–13.13); and

  (10) the future of the doctrine (13.14).

## 13.2  The parties to a challenge

### 13.2.1  *Court proceedings used for challenging decisions*

Challenges to decisions are made in court proceedings between the parties such as the following:

    (1) an application for an injunction, which, as well as being a court order stopping the reference can also be used to stop further performance of the contract following the decision; or

    (2) an application for an order for specific performance, which is a court order that the decision be put into effect—eg, a sale of property at an expert's valuation; or

(3) defence to court proceedings brought to enforce the decision; or

(4) an application to strike out either side's claim under RSC Ord 18 r 19; or

(5) a construction summons, which is an application to the court for a ruling on an allegedly ambiguous document; but see 13.9; or

(6) a petition under s 459 of the Companies Act 1985, on which see the discussion at 3.7.

An application for a declaration can accompany any of the above.

### 13.2.2   Challenging the expert

Challenging the expert by suing him for negligence, where it is the expert, rather than the decision which is being challenged, is dealt with in Chapter 14.

### 13.2.3   Limitation

An action to challenge a decision must, generally, be brought within six years of the decision where the contract to refer to the expert is under hand and twelve in the unlikely case of its being under seal: ss 5 and 8 of the Limitation Act 1980. An expert's decision is probably not an 'award' within s 7 of the Limitation Act 1980. Time runs from the date of the breach, which will probably be no later than the date of the publication of the decision. Where the decision has been obtained by fraud the limitation period may be extended by s 32 of the Limitation Act 1980.

## 13.3   Grounds for challenge

### 13.3.1   Fraud, partiality and mistake

The courts have always said that *fraud* (or *dishonesty*) and *partiality* are valid reasons for refusing to uphold an expert's decision. Much more controversy has been generated by the question of whether a *mistake* also qualifies as a reason, and, more particularly, how serious the mistake has to be. The court approaches the question by looking at the wording of the contract and whether the expert's work has followed what the parties had agreed.

## 13.3.2   Few authorities on fraud and partiality

There are no reported cases of decisions set aside because of fraud or partiality. On the analogy of arbitration law, partiality would have to be actual bias, and not conflicts of interest or apparent lack of independence: see Mustill and Boyd, p 249. For an example of an unsuccessful allegation of partiality, see *Midland Montagu Leasing (UK) Ltd v Tyne & Wear Passenger Transport Executive and Ernst & Whinney* (1990) unreported, Chancery Division, 23 February discussed at 11.6.2.

However, in *Re Boswell & Co (Steels) Ltd* (1989) 5 BCC 145 an auditor's lack of independence was relied on as one of the reasons to make an order under s 459 of the Companies Act 1985 (see 3.7). The evidence of the lack of independence was the auditor's involvement in certain transactions to which the company had been a party; the petitioner failed to obtain details of these transactions and then proceeded to petition to be bought out of the company. The concern for independence shown by the court in this case is an interesting development, but it arose in circumstances where the court has a discretion to exercise statutory powers. The principle probably does not apply in cases where the court does not have those powers.

## 13.3.3   Invalidity

The reference may be invalid because there has been no agreement between the parties that it should take place. An example of this can be found in *Darlington Borough Council v Waring & Gillow (Holdings) Ltd* [1988] 2 EGLR 159, discussed at 10.4.2. The courts will also refuse to enforce a decision if that decision is unclear *Hopcraft v Hickman* (1824) 2 Sim & St 130 or inconclusive: see 13.7.7 below.

## 13.3.4   Revocation of expert's authority

One party to the reference cannot challenge the decision by revoking the authority of the expert without the consent of the other party: the purported revocation would be a repudiation of the agreement to refer. Under the general law of contract (on which see *Chitty on Contracts*, Chapter 24) repudiation gives the other party the right to treat the contract as being at an end and to claim damages for wrongful termination: the alternative right to insist on performance would be meaningless in this context.

There is a statutory provision about the position of arbitrators: under s 1 of the Arbitration Act 1950, the authority of an arbitrator is said to be irrevocable, but it may be revoked with leave of the court.

### 13.3.5 Illegality

The court will not enforce a decision if it would be illegal: *Parken v Whitby* (1823) Turn & R 367.

### 13.3.6 Expert appointed who cannot act

The court will set aside a decision if it is taken by someone who is not or cannot be appointed as the expert. In *Jones (M) v Jones (R R)* [1971] 1 WLR 840 an agreed court order said that the liquidator of a company was to appoint any expert he might select to value the company's machinery. The liquidator valued the machinery himself, and the court gave a declaration that this was contrary to the agreement, and therefore of no effect.

### 13.3.7 Jurisdiction arguments

Opportunities for challenge based on arguments about jurisdiction can survive a reference and prevent an expert's decision being enforced. A reference may be controversial from the start, with allegations that the question referred for decision is outside the terms of the expert clause: if a reference is outside the scope of the expert's jurisdiction, there it will stay, and the issue will be unaffected by an expert having purported to make a decision about it. There may be scope for similar challenges to an expert's decision arising from other aspects of the contract between the parties: for instance, the conditions precedent to the right to refer a dispute to an expert may not have been met, in which case the entire reference will be premature. Serious difficulties can arise when a contract is varied without proper consideration of the effect of the variation on the expert clause. Arguments of this kind can provide effective defences to enforcement proceedings. Appointing authorities take no responsiblity for the validity of their appointments in this regard: see 10.7.2.

## 13.4  Mistake: earlier history

### 13.4.1 An old problem

The law of mistake in expert determination has been kept separate from the general law of contractual mistake, on which see *Chitty on Contracts*, Chapter 5. Judgments on mistake in expert determination point up the conflict between the parties' agreement that a decision shall be final and the injustice of enforcing a defective decision. This conflict is apparent from the earliest case reports. In *Belchier v Reynolds* (1754) 3 Keny 87 at 88 the court said that differences in the valuation of an estate could never be a reason to set the valuation aside, and ordered specific performance, but, as it was 'a hard case on the defendants', ordered each party to bear its own costs.

### 13.4.2 *Early attempts at a solution*

The nineteenth century judges sought to define mistake (or 'miscarriage'). In *Collier v Mason* (1858) 25 Beav 200, Lord Eldon was cited for the principle that

... the court ... must act on the valuation unless there be proof of some mistake or improper motive ... as if the valuer has valued something not included or had valued it on a wholly erroneous basis ...

The practical difficulties of applying this principle are apparent from Lord Eldon's judgment in *Emery v Wase* (1803) 8 Ves Jun 506, where the difference between valuations of £4,000 and £6,000 was said to warrant judicial suspicion that the valuation had not been made with attention to accuracy: but the case was decided on the basis of the court's duty to protect the property of married women. *Parken v Whitby* (1823) Turn & R 367 is sometimes cited for the proposition that the court will not specifically enforce an agreement where the court believes that the price settled by valuers is considerably below the true value of the property; but the case was decided on the grounds of illegality. Neither case is an authority on how serious a discrepancy or inaccuracy has to be for a challenge on the ground of mistake to succeed. In *Weekes v Gallard* (1869) 21 LT 655, the fact that a property had been valued too low did not stop the court ordering specific performance of the contract of sale at that low valuation.

## 13.5 Mistake: more recent developments

### 13.5.1 Dean v Prince: *examples of mistakes*

The modern law tracks the same issues and offers fresh examples based on the old principle. In *Dean v Prince* [1954] 1 Ch 409, at 419, Lord Evershed MR said that the most obvious case of mistake would be if the valuer omitted altogether to take account of some substantial asset or made a serious arithmetical miscalculation in regard to a single but material part of the whole process. In the same case, at 427, Denning LJ (as he then was) gave more examples in the following passage and summarised the circumstances in which he thought the court would interfere:

> ... if the expert added up his figures wrongly; or took something into account which he ought not to have taken into account, or conversely: or interpreted the agreement wrongly: or proceeded on some erroneous principle. In all these cases the court will interfere. Even if the court cannot point to the actual error, nevertheless, if the figure is so extravagantly large or so inadequately small that the only conclusion is that he must have gone wrong somewhere, then the court will interfere in much the same way as the Court of Appeal will interfere with an award of damages if it is a wholly erroneous estimate. These cases about valuers bear some analogy with cases on domestic tribunals, except of course that there need not be a hearing. On matters of opinion, the courts will not interfere; but for mistake of jurisdiction or of principle, and for mistake of law, including interpretation of documents, and for miscarriage of justice, the courts will interfere: see *Lee v Showmen's Guild of Great Britain* [1952] 2 QB 329.

Later sections of this chapter will show how much of this approach has now been discarded: practically every principle contained in it has been reversed.

The expression 'miscarriage of justice' in the last sentence of the extract from the judgment is interesting for two reasons. First, it may explain the meaning of the word 'miscarriage' used in the nineteenth century cases for mistake and, secondly, it raises the public policy issue discussed in Chapter 17. Lord Denning's remarks in *Lee v Showmen's Guild* are quoted at 17.3.5.

### 13.5.2 *Wrong basis of valuation*

In *Jones (M) v Jones (R R)* [1971] 1 WLR 840, a company's factory premises and shops were valued on a break-up basis when the contract called for valuation on a going concern basis. This was held to be a mistake sufficient to overturn the decision.

### 13.5.3 Campbell v Edwards

However, in *Campbell v Edwards* [1976] 1 WLR 403, Lord Denning MR seemed to exclude mistake altogether, except in the case of 'speaking decisions' (on which see 13.7). The case was about a challenge to a surveyor's valuation of the surrender price for a lease. The surveyor was duly appointed by the parties under the lease. The surveyor's price had been £10,000, but the tenant later found two more surveyors who said that the price should be much lower, £3,500 and £1,250 respectively. The Court of Appeal dismissed the tenant's appeal and held that the parties were bound by the honest valuation fixed by the agreed valuer. Lord Denning said, at 407:

It is simply the law of contract. If two persons agree that the price of property should be fixed by a valuer on whom they agree, and he gives that valuation honestly and in good faith, they are bound by it. Even if he has made a mistake they are still bound by it. The reason is because they have agreed to be bound by it. If there were fraud or collusion, of course, it would be very different. Fraud or collusion unravels everything.

It is clear from later passages in the judgment (408B) that Lord Denning had very much in mind the recent changes in the law making a valuer liable in negligence: see 14.5.

Although this case was not cited in the *Imperial Foods Ltd Pension Scheme* case [1986] 1 WLR 717, the court came to a similar conclusion: see 4.3.

### 13.5.4 Baber v Kenwood

The primacy of the law of contract in assessing challenges to experts' decisions was reaffirmed by Sir David Cairns in *Baber v Kenwood Manufacturing Co Ltd and Whinney Murray & Co* [1978] 1 Lloyd's Rep 175 at 181. He said:

... whether a valuation ... is binding ... must depend on the terms of the contract (including any implied terms), on the nature of any circumstances relied on to vitiate the valuation, and the nature of the proceedings on which the issue arises. If the valuation has not been made in accordance with the express terms of the contract then it is clearly not binding. If it is made in accordance with the express terms, the next question is whether there were any implied terms that have not been complied with. Here there may arise a conflict between two principles, one that the court will not imply a term unless it is one which reasonable men would obviously have agreed to if their minds had been directed to the point, the other that a contract should if possible be interpreted in such a way as to achieve fairness between the parties ... mistake is a much more difficult problem ... [than fraud or partiality].

With the other members of the Court of Appeal in that case, he followed *Campbell v Edwards* (cited at 13.5.3).

### 13.5.5 *Robust refusal to intervene*

The Judicial Committee of the Privy Council considered a disputed rent review with a valuer acting as an expert in *Hudson (A)*

*Pty Ltd v Legal & General Life of Australia Ltd* [1986] 2 EGLR 130. The question was whether part of the floor area should be included and if so at what price. The tenants preferred to use the contentious area as air space for the benefit of the lower ground floor rather than selling space for the benefit of the ground floor. The Privy Council upheld the valuer's determination in favour of the landlords, with the comment that there was no discernible mistake in the valuation either in fact or in law. Lord Templeman was not prepared to consider the kinds of mistake which might justify interference by the court with the valuation of an expert, and made the following remark:

In general [we] consider that it would be a disservice to the law and to litigants to encourage forensic attacks on valuations by experts where those attacks are based on textual criticisms more appropriate to the measured analysis of fiscal legislation.

### 13.5.6   *Expert's decision binding on matters of opinion*

An expert surveyor's valuation of development land was alleged to contain fundamental errors in *Campbell and Palmer v Crest Homes (Wessex) Ltd* (1989) unreported, Chancery Division, 13 November. The allegations were all based on the opinion of another expert surveyor and related to what matters should or should not be taken into consideration. The judge said it was quite impossible to say that any error was shown by these matters on the face of the determination, and that the parties were, on a matter of opinion, bound by the opinion of their chosen expert.

## 13.6   Mistake: the present position

### 13.6.1   *A further retreat by the courts*

The current law is contained in the Court of Appeal's judgment in *Jones v Sherwood Computer Services plc* [1991] NPC 60, in which the judgment was delivered in December 1989, and *Nikko Hotels (UK) Ltd v MEPC plc* [1991] 28 EG 86 (discussed at 13.6.8). The non-interventionist trend has been significantly intensified.

### 13.6.2   Jones v Sherwood

In *Jones v Sherwood* (cited at 13.6.1) there was a sale and purchase agreement with part of the consideration deferred. Payment of that deferred consideration depended on the amount by which the acquired company's sales exceeded a certain figure.

The vendor's and the purchaser's accountants were then to review the sales figure and try to agree it with each other: and, if they disagreed, which they did, a third accountant was to determine the figure. All the accountants in the case were said to be acting as experts and not as arbitrators, and the determination was to be final and binding for all purposes.

### 13.6.3 Expert accountants appointed

The plaintiff vendors sought to set aside the expert's decision and to have the court decide the matter, but the defendant purchasers said that the plaintiffs could not do that because the contract bound them to accept the expert's decision. The plaintiffs' accountants were Deloitte, Haskins & Sells and the defendants' accountants were Peat, Marwick, Mitchell. Deloittes thought that two categories of transaction should be included as sales, but Peats thought they should not be included. The expert firm then appointed was Coopers & Lybrand, who set out their terms of reference in some detail, including the difference of opinion between Deloittes and Peats and its financial effect.

### 13.6.4 The decision

Coopers' determination was a brief letter referring to the sale agreement and what they had been asked to determine, and stating the answer: 'We determine that the sales amount to £2,527,135'.

The plaintiffs said this letter was a nullity because the sale agreement had called for a 'report', but the Court of Appeal did not agree that the use of the word 'report' required the expert to set out the reasoning or calculations which led to the conclusion.

### 13.6.5 'Mistakes of mixed fact and law'

By referring back to the earlier documents it was obvious that Coopers had agreed with Peats and disagreed with Deloittes. It did not follow that Coopers reached the same conclusion as Peats by following the same reasoning. The plaintiffs' case was that Peats and Coopers had made mistakes of mixed fact and law, and that they were entitled to ask the court to determine whether or not Coopers had made those mistakes.

### 13.6.6 Coopers' determination upheld

The Court of Appeal considered what sort of mistakes would be sufficient to upset an expert's decision. They said that if the expert departed from his instructions in a material respect, eg where he was called on to value shares in a company and he valued the wrong number of shares or shares in the wrong company, that would be sufficient. The court also cited with approval the example of *Jones v Jones* (cited at 13.6.1 above). In these cases either party would be able to say that the certificate was not binding because the expert had not done what he was appointed to do. The Court of Appeal held that Coopers had not made mistakes of this type. They had determined the sales, and that is what they had been asked to do. The Court of Appeal said that the plaintiffs would have had the right to review Coopers' decision only if there could be implied into the original agreement words describing this kind of challenge which qualified the 'final and binding' description of the decision in the appropriate manner.

### 13.6.7 An investigation by the court would involve 'yet more accountants'

The Court of Appeal in *Jones v Sherwood* (cited at 13.6.1) also addressed the practical problem of how the alleged mistake could be rectified by the court. 'Yet more accountants' would have been needed to give expert evidence. The only way for the court to decide on a matter of accountancy opinion is to obtain the expert evidence of accountants acting as expert witnesses: see 6.7.2.

### 13.6.8 Asking the right questions

In *Nikko v MEPC* (cited at 13.6.1), the judge said that an expert's decision cannot be challenged unless it could be shown that the expert had not performed the task assigned to him. If he had answered the right question in the wrong way, his decision would be binding. If he had answered the wrong question, his decision would be a nullity. The judge went on to say that this would be the case for any dispute whether of fact or law, and that there was no rule of public policy preventing parties from agreeing to remit a question of law to the exclusive and final jurisdiction of an expert.

### 13.6.9 'Judge-proof'

It is therefore hardly surprising that the expression 'judge-proof' is now being applied to experts' decisions as in Jonathan Gaunt QC's article cited in Further Reading: see also Chapter 17.

### 13.7  Speaking and non-speaking decisions

*13.7.1  Definition*

The decision of an expert may be known either as 'speaking' or 'non-speaking'. A speaking decision is one which gives the reasons and calculations behind the decision, whereas a non-speaking decision does not. The expressions are also used with the words certificates, decisions, determinations and valuations, and are sometimes found in describing whether reasons accompany an arbitration award; and an expert decision is often referred to as an award. Hence the expressions 'speaking award' and 'non-speaking award' can be used to describe expert decisions or arbitration awards.

*13.7.2  Speaking decisions previously more vulnerable*

Until 1989 the courts had said that a 'speaking' decision could be upset if it contained an obvious error. Thus, if the decision gave its reasons or calculations, and there were obvious errors in them, the decision could be set aside. A speaking decision was overturned in *Johnston v Chestergate Hat Manufacturing Co Ltd* [1915] 2 Ch 338, where the auditors' certificate showed that the amount due was calculated according to the wrong principle.

*13.7.3  Should the alleged mistake be apparent in the decision?*

The question of whether the existence of a mistake has to be apparent from a speaking decision was raised in *Dean v Prince* [1953] Ch 590, where, at first instance, the judge held that he could look at documents other than the auditors' certificate and the balance sheet and that cross-examination of the auditors would be allowed. (The point was not considered in the appeal at [1954] 1 Ch 409). However, in *Mayne Nickless v Solomon* [1980] Qd R 171, the court held that the mistake must appear from a reading of the decision and not from cross-examination of the valuer.

*13.7.4  Burgess v Purchase*

*Johnston v Chestergate* (cited at 13.7.2) was the principal authority relied on in *Burgess v Purchase & Sons (Farms) Ltd* [1983] Ch 216, where auditors explained how their valuation of the shares in question had been arrived at. Nourse J (as he then was) took the view that the decision itself had to provide evidence of error, without assistance from cross-examination, and that in this case there was sufficient evidence. The merits of the plaintiff's objections to the means of valuation do not appear from the report, and did not need to, because this was a striking-out application under RSC Ord 18, r 19, which allows no evidence to be heard about the case that the plaintiff wished to make.

### 13.7.5 Apus v Farrow

The speaking decision of a surveyor acting as an expert was pronounced to be a nullity in *Apus Properties Ltd v Douglas Henry Farrow Ltd* [1989] NPC 38. His decision stated he had made assumptions about the lease which were held to be incorrect, and those errors resulted in the premises being valued on a fundamentally wrong basis.

### 13.7.6 An unreal distinction

The current law on speaking and non-speaking decisions is to be found in the Court of Appeal's judgment in *Jones v Sherwood Computer Services plc* [1991] NPC 60. Dillon LJ doubted the distinction between the two sorts of decisions: 'Even speaking valuations may say much or little; they may be voluble or taciturn if not wholly dumb.' The real question was whether they provided material for assisting challenges to the decision before the court, by way of evidence of what the expert had done and why he had done it. *Burgess v Purchase* (cited at 13.7.4) was disapproved. It therefore follows that it is no longer good law that a speaking decision may be challenged, but that a non-speaking decision may not be. Each decision must be examined to see what it discloses.

### 13.7.7 Effect of qualifying words

What is the effect of a speaking decision which contains words which could be said to qualify the decision? This question was considered by Knox J in *Midland Montagu Leasing (UK) Ltd v Tyne & Wear Passenger Transport Executive and Ernst & Whinney* (1990) unreported, Chancery Division, 23 February. A finance leasing agreement said that the auditors for the owners acting as experts 'shall ... conclusively certify ... [the rental].' The auditors said in their certificate that they had used one 'methodology' rather than another and that it was not clear from the clause in the lease which methodology they should use. In the certificate the auditor did not just recite the clause: he specifically raised the methodology point. He was later asked to delete the qualification from his certificate, and refused. The court found that the certificate was conclusive. (The court also looked at the methodology and decided that the expert had been right about it anyway.) The adverb 'conclusively' qualifying the word 'certify' may be no more than the more commonly encountered provision that the expert's decision will be final. On that assumption it is clearly, subject to the precise words used, likely to be a contractual obligation, binding the expert and the parties, that the decision be final. If a certificate is found not to be conclusive or final when the contract or terms of reference say it should be, that finding will provide good grounds for challenge. In *Shorrock Ltd v Meggitt plc* [1991] BCC 471, qualifying words rendered a certificate inconclusive and therefore invalid. Auditors certified the amount of the net deficit of a company under the terms of an agreement for the sale and purchase of that company, but stated that they were unable to determine the adequacy or otherwise of a provision made by the directors in respect of potential legal claims against the company. The Court of Appeal said:

It was open to the ... auditors to certify that the ... deficit was [a particular figure] or, if they felt unable to do that, to refuse to certify. But I do not think it was open to them to state a sum constituting the ... deficit and then say in effect they were not sure if the sum was correct. That defeats the whole purpose of requiring a certificate, since it destroys the certainty which the parties required by providing for the certificate.

This case also established the important principle that issues about the validity of certificates are a matter of construction of the agreements under which the certificates are to be given, and not issues that can be determined with the assistance of evidence from expert witnesses.

### 13.7.8 Reasons

Can the expert be compelled to produce reasons for his decision? This would have the effect of either:

(1) turning a 'non-speaking' decision into a 'speaking' one, where the expert had not been specifically instructed beforehand to produce a speaking decision; or

(2) giving more detail to an existing 'speaking' decision.

In the latter context, Peter Gibson J regarded this prospect 'with some alarm' in *Campbell and Palmer v Crest Homes (Wessex) Ltd* (1989) unreported, Chancery Division, 13 November. He said that he could not believe that it should be easier to challenge a reasoned award issued by an expert than a reasoned award issued by an arbitrator. The court has not encouraged applications under s 1(5) of the Arbitration Act 1979 for orders that arbitrators give reasons: *Universal Petroleum v Handels und Transport GmbH* [1987] 1 WLR 1178. It is therefore very unlikely that the court would insist on an expert giving reasons where it had not been agreed beforehand that he would. However, where an expert had agreed to give his decisions and produced none, presumably the court would view an application more favourably, on the ground that the expert was in breach of contract.

## 13.8 Points of law

### 13.8.1 Has the expert asked the right question?

The effect of the recent decisions is that points of law cannot now be relied on for challenges. The parties have to accept the expert's decision, unless he has asked himself the wrong question of law: *Nikko Hotels (UK) Ltd v MEPC plc* [1991] 28 EG 86.

### 13.8.2 An attempt to stop an expert taking legal advice

The Court of Appeal had taken a similar line in *Chelsea Man plc v Vivat Holdings plc* (1989) unreported, Court of Appeal, 24 August. The plaintiffs were seeking an injunction to stop a reference to an expert proceeding. Their complaint was that the accountancy expert was going to interpret the agreement, which was a matter of law, and that he had announced that he would be assisted by a law firm. The plaintiffs said that interpretation of the agreement could only be a matter for the court. The court said that the parties had chosen the manner by which they wished to have their disputes resolved, and that the wording of the clause did not leave any scope for saying that, in so far as that matter was one of law, it was to be determined not by the expert but by the court.

### 13.8.3 How should the expert resolve points of law?

The manner in which the point of law is to be decided is a matter for agreement between the parties and the expert. In *Chelsea Man v Vivat* (cited at 13.8.2) a law firm was to be consulted. In *Nikko v MEPC* (cited at 13.8.1) the expert arranged for the point of law to be decided as a preliminary issue at a formal hearing at which he was addressed by counsel and himself assisted by a Queen's Counsel. Whichever way a point of law is resolved, including without lawyers being consulted, a decision on a point of law will stand unless the expert has asked himself the wrong question of law.

### 13.8.4   Ousting the jurisdiction of the court?

The wider issues raised by this are discussed in Chapter 17.

## 13.9   Construction of documents

### 13.9.1   Construction issues may involve considerable investigation

Interpretation or 'construction' of the documents setting out the manner in which the expert should have resolved the issue appeared, until recently, to be a fruitful line for challenge to decisions. In *Arco British Ltd v Sun Oil Britain Ltd* (1988) unreported, Court of Appeal, 14 December, the courts investigated the technology of oil fields in some detail for the purpose of constructing the agreement: see further 7.2.4. Both parties accepted that the court had jurisdiction to do this despite the expert clause.

### 13.9.2   Construction now left to experts

However, this line of challenge has been closed down by *Nikko Hotels (UK) Ltd v MEPC plc* [1991] 28 EG 86, which allows challenges only if the expert has asked himself the wrong question, including a question of law. Construction of documents is a matter of law because of the common law tradition. This was explained by Lord Diplock in *Pioneer Shipping Ltd v BTP Tioxide Ltd*, AC 1982 724 at 736, where he said that the English system treated the construction of written agreements as questions of law because of the legacy of trial by juries who might not all be literate. The context of these remarks was his preference for allowing arbitrators to make final decisions on questions of construction. *Nikko v MEPC* applies that preference to experts' decisions. An expert can now make a final determination about the construction of documents provided he asks himself the right question.

### 13.9.3   Raise construction issues early

Construction issues can still be raised before the reference has got under way: 8.17.1 and 11.2.

## 13.10 Specific instructions for the expert

### 13.10.1 Examples

Expert clauses and terms of reference may characterise the decision the expert is to make by the use of certain adjectives or longer, more elaborate qualifications. For instance, a clause providing for auditors to value shares may state that the auditor is to certify their 'fair value' or similar words (see 3.5); a minority holding of shares is to be valued without regard to the fact that it is a minority holding (see 3.6); surveyors have to assume certain facts and disregard others in establishing a rental (see 2.3.3).

### 13.10.2 Unlikely to assist challenges

Specific instructions of this type are unlikely to provide material for challenge because of:

(1) the policy of the court in allowing final determination by experts on all matters including construction of documents (see 13.9) and

(2) the practice of experts not to issue decisions accompanied by reasons (see 14.7.7).

## 13.11 'In the absence of manifest error'

Expert clauses often provide that the decision is to be final and binding in the absence of manifest error. This raises the question whether these words widen the scope for challenge. Is there any difference between 'error' and 'mistake'? There appears to be no authority on the point, but they would probably not be understood differently, in view of the court's use of the word 'erroneous' in *Jones (M) v Jones (R R)* [1971] 1 WLR 840. The word 'manifest' presumably means 'obvious' in today's language. The likely result is that this wording does no more than track the law as laid down in *Jones v Sherwood Computer Services plc* [1991] NPC 60: see 13.6.

## 13.12 Consequence of a mistaken decision

### 13.12.1 Is a new valuation needed?

In *Jones v Jones* (see 13.11) the court considered what the fate should be of a valuation 'made on an erroneous principle'. The court said that there was no general rule that a valuation made on an 'erroneous principle' (which presumably means the same as a mistaken decision) had to stand unless it were also shown that a valuation on the right principle would produce a materially different figure from the figure of the erroneous valuation: if there were such a rule, it would place on the objector the extra burden of making a fresh valuation which in its turn might also be rejected. Thus a valuation or any other kind of decision made on an erroneous principle should fall with proof that the principle is erroneous.

### 13.12.2 The mistake may not vitiate the decision

In *Frank H Wright (Constructions) Ltd v Frodoor Ltd* [1967] 1 WLR 506 a valuation stated that some assets had not been included, when in fact they had been, but the result was still the same and completely unaffected by this error; there was therefore no need for the court to correct the valuation.

### 13.12.3 The court can fill the gap

The court will usually be able to supply the right valuation or decision in substitution for one found incorrect: *Sudbrook Trading Estate Ltd v Eggleton* [1983] AC 444: and see 10.3.3.

### 13.13 Procedural unfairness

### 13.13.1 A ground for challenge?

Sometimes the expert's procedures are believed by a party to have been unfair. Is the failure to follow a fair procedure a ground for challenging the decision?

### 13.13.2 A breach of contract

In *Capricorn Inks Pty Ltd v Lawter International (Australasia) Pty Ltd* [1989] 1 Qd R 8, accountants appointed to assess damages were held to have acted in excess of jurisdiction by not acting with procedural fairness. Their terms of reference were contained in a letter written on behalf of both parties. The accountants' error lay in receiving and acting upon a further claim which had not been in their terms of reference and had not been notified to the other party. That further claim increased the figure from A$ 50,000 to A$ 212,796. The accountants' contract with the parties was to assess damages claimed in the terms of reference. They broke that contract by taking the later (and much larger) claim into account.

*13.13.3 Can a serious breach be shown?*

Claims based on procedural unfairness will therefore succeed if the unfairness can be shown to be a serious breach of contract.

## 13.14 The future of 'mistake'

*13.14.1 Mistakes that are sufficiently serious are not the real problem*

It is difficult to predict how the court will react to future challenges on the grounds of mistake. Examples of the type of mistake thought sufficiently serious by the Court of Appeal to warrant challenge in *Jones v Sherwood* (see 13.6) were valuing shares in the wrong company and valuing the wrong number of shares. This is unlikely to be the type of mistake that should occur: and, if it did occur, the other party would more readily accept it as a mistake making the decision invalid.

*13.14.2 Construction arguments no longer available*

*Nikko v MEPC* (see 13.8) has closed off what seemed to be the remaining possibility for challenge on the grounds of the expert's construction of the documents.

*13.14.3 Procedural unfairness may be a ground for challenge*

*Capricorn v Lawter* (see 13.13.2) may provide openings for challenge on procedure.

*13.14.4 The court will continue not to intervene*

That leaves difficult cases where an expert has reached a decision which is widely believed to be incorrect but cannot be challenged. Current trends will favour making the parties live with it. In *Northern Regional Health Authority v Derek Crouch Construction Co Ltd* [1984] 1 QB 644, the Court of Appeal held that the courts do not have jurisdiction over certain types of building disputes because of the wording of the arbitration clause in the construction industry's standard form contracts, and that the court should not alter agreed machinery for resolving disputes where that machinery has not broken down. This controversial decision has led to a great deal of difficulty; but the decision demonstrates the current trend in arbitration which, like references to experts, is another form of machinery for resolving disputes outside the court. The court will therefore tend not to intervene. A similar attitude was taken to another example of agreed machinery for resolving disputes, a liquidated damages clause, in *Temloc v Errill Properties Ltd* (1989) 39 BLR 30: see 17.2.2.

# Chapter 14

# Rights and Duties of Experts

## 14.1 Summary

This chapter considers:
(1) experts' rights to fees and expenses (14.2);
(2) arbitral immunity for experts pre–1975 (14.3);
(3) the change in the law on certifiers' liability (14.4);
(4) the current law under which experts are not immune (14.5);
(5) the obsolete concept of the 'quasi-arbitrator' (14.6);
(6) the liability of experts for professional negligence (14.7);
(7) three alleged duties of experts (14.7–14.10); and
(8) the liability of experts in tort (14.11).

## 14.2 Fees and expenses

### 14.2.1 Contract establishes the right to be paid

An expert has no right to receive fees for his work or payment of his expenses unless that right is established by agreement with the parties. Thus the law of contract will govern his entitlement to collect fees and expenses from either or both of the parties, or from some third party; and it will also govern the amount of the fees and expenses. An expert who does not ensure that the question of fees and expenses is determined in advance might, if the question were subsequently disputed, have to sue both to establish the fact that he was owed money (either as a matter of contract or *quantum meruit*) and to justify the amount.

### 14.2.2 Should be decided along with other terms of reference

While the expert clause itself may lay down that the parties are to be responsible for the fees and expenses of the expert in equal shares, which is quite common, or that they are to be met by some other party (see 8.12), the clause itself may not be sufficient to establish the expert's entitlement unless its terms are clearly incorporated into the expert's contract to conduct the reference. In any case, the amounts of the fees and expenses are still likely to be at large, because expert clauses never lay down the amounts, except in the case of fees by the use of a percentage of the amount at issue, and expenses cannot be considered before a reference. The expert will therefore wish to have the question of fees and expenses agreed with the parties in the terms of reference: see 11.4.2.

### 14.2.3 Calculating the fees

The amount of the expert's fees will depend on negotiation, unless it has been established by the expert clause. The amount will be determined either by a percentage, a fixed sum arrived at on some other basis, or an hourly rate. It is unusual to see hourly rates spelled out in terms of reference, but it may save arguments later. The expert should bear in mind that the parties may settle the matter before he has completed his work.

### 14.2.4 No procedure for control

There is no specific procedure for control by the courts of the amount of an expert's fees, as there is with arbitrators under s 19 of the Arbitration Act 1950. If an expert sues for his fees, the entitlement and/or the amount could be challenged in court only by reference to the contract made by the parties about the fees. Questions about the reasonableness of the amount charged would arise only if the concept was part of that contract.

### 14.2.5 Entitlement to expenses also a matter of contract

The expert's expenses such as seeking outside legal advice will generally be recoverable only if the parties have agreed to the expense.

### 14.2.6 No entitlement if reference invalid

An expert may have no entitlement to fees and expenses if the reference itself is invalid, as appears to have been the consequence in *Darlington Borough Council v Waring & Gillow (Holdings) Ltd* [1988] 2 EGLR 159, discussed at 10.4.2. An expert would be sure to be paid only if he had included a provision in his agreement with the parties that they would pay his fees even if the reference turned out to be invalid for this or whatever reason.

### 14.2.7 Securing payment

An expert may find it necessary to take steps to secure the payment of fees and expenses by, for instance, making payment of his fees a condition of publishing his decision.

### 14.2.8 Limitation

There is a six-year limitation period for collecting fees and expenses, unless the expert is appointed under seal in which case it is twelve years: ss 5 and 8 of the Limitation Act 1980.

## 14.3 Arbitral immunity for experts until 1975

### 14.3.1 Pappa v Rose

A number of attempts to sue experts reached the law reports in the years before 1975, but they invariably met the answer that the experts were 'quasi-arbitrators' and therefore could not be sued. In *Pappa v Rose* (1872) LR 7 CP 525, a broker deciding whether raisins were 'fair average quality' in his opinion was held to be 'in the position of a quasi-arbitrator' or 'in the nature of an arbitrator'. The broker was said to have acted honestly and in good faith, and that was all that was required of him. There was no implied contract that he would have any degree of skill. (For a discussion of the meaning of 'quasi-arbitrator' see 14.6 below.)

### 14.3.2 Jenkins v Betham

For Mr Rose to escape liability, the courts had to distinguish *Jenkins v Betham* (1855) 15 CB 167. Two differences were identified: the first was what stage the dispute, if any, had reached, and the second was the professed ability of the defendants. In *Jenkins v Betham* two valuers of ecclesiastical property had been appointed, one to advise the representatives of a deceased rector, the other to advise the incoming rector. The incoming rector's valuers were incompetent and ignorant of the subject, and caused their client loss. There was an implied term in that contract that the valuers were qualified to act and understood the subject, and the valuers were in breach. The matter never proceeded to what was then called 'umpirage', ie the appointment by the party-appointed valuers of an umpire and his consideration of the matter. The court at first instance in *Pappa v Rose* (1871) LR 7 CP 32 thought it significant that 'umpirage' had not been reached because in its view there could be no real dispute before that stage. The appeal court in *Pappa v Rose* (1872) LR 7 CP 525 noted that the valuers in *Jenkins v Betham* had declared themselves to be persons possessed of proper skill for valuations of ecclesiastical property, whereas Mr Rose was only a selling broker expressing his opinion.

### 14.3.3   Tharsis Sulphur v Loftus

In *Tharsis Sulphur & Copper Co Ltd v Loftus* (1872) LR 8 CP 1 the court decided that an average adjuster appointed under a contract to determine cargo damage was also 'in the nature of an arbitrator' between the parties, and followed *Pappa v Rose* (cited at 14.3.1).

### 14.3.4   Turner v Goulden

*Turner v Goulden* (1873) LR 9 CP 57 was similar to *Jenkins v Betham* (cited at 14.3.2). The plaintiff asked the defendant to value a bookselling business that he wished to purchase. The defendant met the vendor's valuer and agreed the valuation of the goodwill on what the plaintiff alleged was the wrong basis. The court allowed the action to proceed, because the procedure was a valuation and not an arbitration.

### 14.3.5   Architects' certificates

An architect certifying amounts payable to a contractor under a building contract was held to be in the position of an arbitrator in *Stevenson v Watson* (1879) 4 CP 148 and therefore not liable to the contractor, and, by a considerable extension of the same argument, not liable to the employer either in *Chambers v Goldthorpe* [1901] 1 KB 624. The judgment in *Chambers v Goldthorpe* gave a prominent role to the influential concept of a professional 'holding the scales' between the parties.

### 14.3.6   Surveyors' valuations

In *Boynton v Richardson's* [1924] WN 262, the court said that surveyors appointed under a contract to value timber had to 'hold the scales' between the two parties and were quasi-arbitrators, and had to be able to exercise their judgment free from the embarrassment of a possible action for negligence. A similar line was taken in *O'Brien v Perry & Daw* (1941) 85 SJ 142.

## 14.3.7 Finnegan v Allen

In *Finnegan v Allen* [1943] 1 KB 425, the Court of Appeal struck out a claim against an accountant who, it was alleged, had not valued shares in accordance with the instructions in the agreement under which he had been appointed. The court did not inquire into the nature of his departure from the instructions, and said that as a quasi-arbitrator all he had to to do was to act honestly.

## 14.4  *Sutcliffe v Thackrah*

### 14.4.1  *Architects lose immunity*

In *Sutcliffe v Thackrah* [1974] AC 727 the House of Lords overruled *Chambers v Goldthorpe* (see 14.3.5), and held that an architect certifying payments due to a contractor under a building contract was liable for professional negligence to his client the employer. It did not follow that, because the architect was under a duty to act fairly in making a valuation for the certificates, he was acting in a judicial capacity and therefore immune from liability to his principal for loss caused to him by a negligent valuation. Lord Reid said (at 736F):

There is modern authority to the effect that if the valuer knows his valuation will affect or bind another person besides his client ... then he can claim an arbitrator's immunity. But why should that be? ... I do not believe a professional man would ... be influenced in any significant way because he knew that the interests of some other person beside his employer would be affected by the conclusion which he reached.

### 14.4.2  *Duty of care owed to non-client*

In the same case, at 758C, Lord Salmon stated that it was generally well established that professionals owed their clients a duty to exercise reasonable skill and care. The 'heresy' was that 'if a person engaged to act for a client ought to act fairly and impartially towards the person with whom his client is dealing, then he is immune from being sued by his client — however negligent he may have been'. Lord Salmon gave as an example two instances of the valuation of a picture, the first for a client who does not tell him the reason for the valuation, and the second where the client tells him the valuation is needed because he is about to sell the picture to a friend. Lord Salmon said he could find no sensible basis for the 'astonishing' proposition that the valuer should be liable for negligence in the first instance, but not in the second.

### 14.4.3   Architects are different from valuers and experts

These arguments were advanced in a case about an architect whose position as the certifier under a building contract is different from the position of a valuer, because the architect's client is the employer under the building contract, and the employer and the contractor do not instruct the architect jointly. However, the similarities were more compelling than the differences: and, by chance, the courts were considering a case of valuer's negligence at the same time.

## 14.5   *Arenson v Casson Beckman*

### 14.5.1   Shares undervalued by a factor of six

In *Arenson v Casson Beckman Rutley & Co* [1975] 3 WLR 815 an agreement provided that shares in a private company had to be sold back to the plaintiff's uncle on the plaintiff leaving the business; the price of the shares was to be the fair value as determined by the company's auditors, whose valuation acting as experts and not as arbitrators was to be final and binding on all parties. The company secretary orally requested the auditors to give a valuation, which they duly did, and the plaintiff sold his shares at that price. The company was floated shortly after that with the shares selling at six times the auditors' valuation. The House of Lords held that the valuer could be liable in negligence. To establish immunity it would be necessary for the valuer to show a 'formulated dispute' (see 15.5) had been put to him to resolve in a judicial manner; or, in other words, that he had been an arbitrator. The decision in *Sutcliffe v Thackrah* (cited at 14.4.1) was very recent, and the Lords justified their view mainly on public policy grounds that the primary rule is that those who commit breaches of a duty of care should be liable to those affected.

### 14.5.2   Duty identical in contract and tort?

Neither the plaintiff nor his uncle had a contract with the auditors. The company secretary had simply passed on an oral instruction. It was not known whether the auditors had charged a fee for their valuation. The Lords did not see these factors made a difference. They saw the duty of the auditor, whether in contract or tort, as identical, following the decision of the House of Lords in *Hedley Byrne & Co Ltd v Heller & Partners Ltd* [1964] AC 465: see further 14.11.

### 14.5.3 Arenson *unchallenged*

The decision in *Arenson* was followed in *Palacath Ltd v Flanagan* [1985] 2 All ER 161. No serious challenge has been mounted to *Arenson*. The only defence usually available to a valuer is that he did not act as an expert, but as an arbitrator in the full sense, and not as a 'quasi-arbitrator', considered in 14.6. Chapter 15 discusses the distinction between experts and arbitrators and sets out the factors for an assessment of which category a referee belongs to.

## 14.6 Quasi-arbitrators

### 14.6.1 *An obsolete status providing immunity for experts*

In many of the cases brought against experts, where full arbitral status did not seem appropriate, the expert's immunity was said to derive from the fact that the expert's status was that of a 'quasi-arbitrator', or that the expert was 'in the position of an arbitrator', or that an expert was 'in the nature of an arbitrator'. The concept seems to have been killed off by *Sutcliffe v Thackrah* (cited at 14.6.4).

### 14.6.2 *Avoiding a definition*

Goddard LJ (as he then was) in *Finnegan v Allen* [1943] 1 KB 425 at 436, said that the distinction between an arbitrator and what the courts have called a quasi-arbitrator was not capable of precise definition. He then gave commodity arbitrations as an example : see 15.6.5–7.

### 14.6.3 *A quasi-arbitrator can represent one of the parties only*

A distinction was drawn between arbitrators and quasi-arbitrators in *Panamena Europea Navigacion (Compania Limitada) v Frederick Leyland & Co Ltd (J Russell & Co)* [1947] AC 428, where the shipowners' surveyor was to certify that repairs had been satisfactorily carried out. The House of Lords held that the surveyor was discharging the duties of both expert and quasi-arbitrator, and was not in the position of an independent arbitrator who had no other duty which involved acting in the interests of one of the parties, and that accordingly in so acting he was not guilty of collusion or bad faith.

## 14.6.4  'Illogical'

In *Sutcliffe v Thackrah* [1974] AC 727 at 737, Lord Reid said:

For some reason not clear to me a theory has developed and is reflected in many decided cases to the effect that where the architect has agreed or is required to act fairly he becomes what has often been called a quasi-arbitrator ... Persons who undertake to act fairly have often been called 'quasi-arbitrators'. One might suppose that to be based on the completely illogical argument—all persons carrying out judicial functions must act fairly, therefore all persons who must act fairly are carrying out judicial functions. There is nothing judicial about an architect's function in determining whether certain work is defective ...

and later, at 738G:

If immunity [of an arbitrator or quasi-arbitrator] is claimed then it is for the person claiming it to shew that the functions in the performance of which he was negligent were sufficiently judicial in character.

Lord Morris said (at 752H):

There may be circumstances in which what was in effect an arbitration is not one that is within the provisions of the Arbitration Act. The expression 'quasi-arbitrator' should only be used in that connection. A person will only be an arbitrator or quasi-arbitrator if there is a submission to him either of a specific dispute or of present points of difference or of defined differences that may in future arise and if there is agreement that his decision will be binding.

## 14.6.5  *Reductio ad absurdum: but really a matter of public policy*

Lord Simon showed what a difficult concept this is when he reviewed various possible definitions of 'quasi-arbitrator' in *Arenson v Casson Beckman Rutley & Co* [1975] 3 WLR 815 at 824 G. He said that it could mean

(1) a third party whose duty it is, in deciding a question, to 'hold the scales fairly' and who is 'likely to be shot at by both sides'—this was formulated three different ways; or

(2) 'an arbitrator at common law in contradistinction from one under the Arbitration Act 1950' [an obscure concept—presumably only for oral arbitration agreements or agreements specifically excluding the operation of the Act]; or

(3) 'a person who is not an arbitrator under the Arbitration Act 1950 but nevertheless "acts in a judicial capacity" or "character" or "fulfills a judicial function".'

Lord Simon said that these definitions were all effectively excluded by *Sutcliffe v Thackrah* (cited at 14.6.4). But he also said that the immunity of arbitrators was a secondary issue of public policy. The primary issue of public policy was the duty to act with care with regard to another person. In the same case, Lord Kilbrandon said (831B): 'I am as mistrustful of the phrase "mere valuer" as I know some of your Lordships are of the office of "quasi-arbitrator"'. The condescending expression 'mere valuer' appears in several of the cases where valuers are contrasted with arbitrators.

### 14.6.6 'Quasi-arbitrator' cannot be defined

Judges in more recent cases have refused to enter the arena. Mars-Jones J in *Palacath Ltd v Flanagan* [1985] 2 All ER 161 decided that a surveyor was not immune without specifically denying that he had acted as a quasi-arbitrator. Scott J (as he then was) in *North Eastern Cooperative Society Ltd v Newcastle upon Tyne City Council* [1987] 1 EGLR 142 said, at 143K:

A declaration that someone was acting as a 'quasi-arbitrator' would be likely itself to be the subject of a future application to the court as to what the declaration meant ...

and, at 146E:

... I do not understand any accurate meaning that can be ascribed to such an expression as 'quasi-arbitrator'.

### 14.6.7 Death of the concept

Let us hope therefore that quasi-arbitrators have made their final appearance. The concept was artificial, being devised in order to give immunity to professionals with more than one client, and incomprehensible.

## 14.7 Liability for professional negligence

### 14.7.1 Professional negligence usually in contract

Since the decision in *Arenson v Casson Beckman Rutley & Co* [1975] 3 WLR 815 the courts have allowed actions for professional negligence against experts. Suing the expert will usually mean bringing a claim for professional negligence. 'Professional negligence' is a generic term covering claims for negligence against professionals, usually for breach of contract. Usually the claimant has a contract with the professional, and experts appointed in recent times are almost invariably professionals.

## 14.7.2   Distinguish the tort of negligence

'Negligence' in this context should be distinguished from the tort of negligence, where the law implies a duty of care between parties who have not made a contract with each other. There are a few occasions where the expert does not have a contract with either or both of the parties, but as the relationship is a close one based on reliance, the expert's liability is likely to be the same as if there had been a contract: see 14.11. However, tortious liability is notoriously difficult to predict, and a contract is much less likely to give rise to wasteful disputes.

## 14.7.3   Claims against experts

A claim against an expert may be that:
(1) he has failed to carry out the reference properly; or
(2) he has failed to deliver a timely decision; or
(3) he has not followed the parties' instructions: or
(4) he has not kept to the standard of skill and care of his profession.

If any of these claims succeeds, an expert may not only lose his right to claim his fees and expenses, but he may also be liable for a damages claim for wasted time and money, depending on whether his actions have caused the loss complained of.

(1) Whether the expert has failed to carry out the reference properly will depend on either the specific instructions given to him or arguments about the implied duties of an expert conducting a reference: for three possible examples, see 14.8, 14.9 and 14.10.

(2) Failure to deliver a decision within a reasonable time will be a breach of the implied duty under s 14 of the Supply of Goods and Services Act 1982, unless there is a specific time provision or the duty has been expressly excluded by agreement with the parties.

(3) Failure to follow instructions should be actionable for breach of contract, although evidence may be difficult to find if the expert issues a non-speaking decision.

(4) For failure to keep to the standard of skill and care of the expert's profession, see 14.7.5.

## 14.7.4   Professional negligence of experts generally

The expression 'professional negligence' is commonly used by lawyers to cover all four categories in 14.7.1 above, except possibly the second one. Relevant aspects of the fourth category are summarised at 14.7.5. For professional negligence generally, see *Professional Negligence* by Jackson and Powell (Sweet and Maxwell, London 1987), and for some unsuccessful attempts to sue experts, see *Belvedere Motors v King* [1981] EGD 850 and *Wallshire Ltd v Aarons* [1989] 1 EGLR 147 (surveyors) and *Whiteoak v Walker* (1988) 4 BCC 122 (auditor).

### 14.7.5 Failure to keep to professional standard

The elements of the fourth category are as follows. The expert probably does not have any separate liability in his secondary profession of being an expert, other than the duties set out in 14.7.3 and 14.8–10. The expert's liability in his primary profession is considered by looking at successful actions against members of the same profession in cases where the duty is owed to one party only: for instance, where a valuation is prepared for a buyer and not both buyer and seller. The standard of competence of a professional was laid down in *Bolam v Friern Hospital Management Committee* [1957] 1 WLR 582 and now in s 13 of the Supply of Goods and Services Act 1982; there is an implied obligation of reasonable skill and care. An expert who claims greater qualifications than he in fact possesses will be judged by the standard he claims: *Wilsher v Essex Area Health Authority* [1987] 2 WLR 425, a point which survived the appeal at [1988] 2 WLR 557. *Wilsher* was considered in *Whiteoak v Walker* (1988) 4 BCC 122, where an auditor was sued for negligence in valuing shares. The court said that in the circumstances of that case the auditor could not have been expected to act as a specialist valuer, and was therefore not liable for failing to reach that higher standard.

### 14.7.6 Excluding liability

Experts naturally look for ways to minimise their exposure to claims: the liability of adjudicators is excluded specifically by the wording of the New Engineering Contract (1991). Experts could seek to exclude the implied duty of skill and care in individual references, but it is not attractive. An exclusion would be subject to the requirement of reasonableness imposed by ss 2 and 3 of the Unfair Contract Terms Act 1977. The implied duty of skill and care is excluded for arbitrators by the Supply of Goods and Services Regulations 1985 (SI 1985 No 1). The terms of this statutory instrument do not extend to arbitrators acting as experts, nor to the failure to deliver a decision within a reasonable time (see 14.7.3).

### 14.7.7   Reluctance to give reasons

Experts prefer to issue 'non-speaking' decisions: ie those not disclosing their reasons. This stems from the fact that the less an expert discloses of his work, the less anyone can find fault with it. The provision of reasons will increase an expert's vulnerability to claims, because the details of the workings and calculations may be the very evidence that would otherwise be lacking. For a discussion of whether an expert can be compelled to give reasons for his decision, see 13.7.8. It is a matter determined by the terms of the expert's contract. It is common in rent review for reasons to be available only if the parties pay the expert higher fees.

### 14.7.8   General dispute resolution

The potential liability of an expert who decides all disputes under a contract, both technical and non-technical, has yet to be considered by the courts. Consider the case of the Sydney shopping complex, set out at 6.9. Does an engineer who decides matters of planning regulations, architectural design and quantification of damages have the same liability for his decisions on those matters as for his decisions on engineering matters, and, if so, on what basis? A construction dispute comprising all those features would, if determined by arbitration or litigation, probably need expert witnesses from four different professional disciplines as well as lawyers. An expert taking on the task of deciding a dispute of this kind would be well advised to establish terms excluding claims.

### 14.7.9   Limitation

The limitation period for claims against experts is six years, unless the expert is appointed under seal, in which case it is twelve: ss 5 and 8 of the Limitation Act 1980. The period in tort may be lengthened by the Latent Damage Act 1986.

## 14.8   A duty to make independent investigations?

### 14.8.1   Does the duty exist?

One of the reasons for referring a question to an expert is that the expert should be sufficiently qualified, if not actually to know the answer, at least to know where to look for it. On the other hand, the parties will usually be only too eager to let him know what they think the answer should be. Is the expert supposed to carry out his own independent investigations beyond the material submitted to him by the parties?

### 14.8.2   What has the expert been asked to do?

This has to be approached by looking at the expert clause and other instructions given to the expert. If there is a specific obligation to carry out independent investigations, the expert would be at fault in not doing so.

### 14.8.3   Is there a need to make an independent investigation?

Where there is no specific provision, the duty will depend on whether the parties have submitted sufficient material on which to make a decision. In *Wallshire Ltd v Aarons* [1989] 1 EGLR 147, it was argued that a surveyor conducting a rent review as an expert should have looked at more evidence of comparable lettings. The court decided that in this case there was already sufficient evidence presented by the parties.

### 14.8.4   The allegation may rebound on the party making it

Thus an expert may need to carry out his own independent investigations if the parties have not submitted adequate material on which to make a decision: and the expert might be liable for professional negligence if he did not do so. Proving that the negligence caused loss is likely to be difficult because of the uncertainty of the results of that independent investigation: and the party making the allegation might have the damages reduced for contributory negligence in not having drawn the matter to the expert's attention during the course of the reference.

### 14.8.5   Arbitrators

By contrast, an arbitrator who carries out his own independent investigation risks removal for misconduct: see 15.6.3.

### 14.8.6   Parties can prevent independent investigations

The parties could agree to prevent the expert from carrying out his own independent investigations, either in the expert clause (8.15.8) or at the start of a reference (11.6.3).

## 14.9   A duty to act fairly?

### 14.9.1   Must each side be allowed a say?

Questions are sometimes raised about the fairness of procedures adopted by experts. Do the procedures allow each side to have its say and know what the other side are saying? The suggested procedure in Appendix A states that each party is to send its submission to the expert and copy it to the other party.

### 14.9.2  Contract law governs the position

The problem arose in an acute form in the Australian case of *Capricorn Inks Pty Ltd v Lawter International (Australasia) Pty Ltd* [1989] 1 Qd R 8. The case is discussed at 13.13.2. Burke and Chinkin in [1989] ICLR 401 ask what the effect would be if the parties required their expert to observe the rules of natural justice. They consider that there is no reason why parties should not expect fair procedures to be followed, and that the public law decision *Ridge v Baldwin* [1964] AC 40 applies the rules of natural justice to any person making a decision about individuals. But the dismissal of a chief constable is very different from a company's claim for damages. There is some support for Burke and Chinkin's view in the remarks of Denning LJ (as he then was) in *Lee v Showmen's Guild of Great Britain* [1952] 2 QB 329 at 342, where he stated that a domestic tribunal must observe the principles of natural justice; but this was in the context of being given a reasonable opportunity to meet a 'charge', in this case the attempt to expel a member from a trade union. There is no authority for saying that the court applies any other rules other than those of contract law when assessing whether an expert's decision shall stand. Conversely, it was argued in *R v Kidderminster District Valuer, ex p Powell* (1991) *The Times*, 23 July, that a valuation made by a district valuer was a matter of private law and not subject to judicial review under RSC Ord 53. The argument was rejected.

### 14.9.3  Codes of conduct will make experts more vulnerable

The question remains whether an expert should be liable to a party for damages for the consequences of procedural unfairness. Burke and Chinkin set out an expert's code of conduct in an appendix to their article cited at 14.9.2. If an expert adopted a code of conduct, it would become part of his contract with the parties and make it much easier for a party to make a claim in the case of a breach. Similarly, a requirement that the expert observe the rules of natural justice could be made a contractual obligation. If no code is adopted or requirement made, the issue will be whether it was an implied term of the contract that the expert would follow fair procedures, which would be difficult to oppose in general terms, but the exact extent of the duty would always be controversial.

### 14.9.4   The duty does exist, but each case will need investigation

An expert, therefore, does have a duty to observe procedural fairness. The matter will be governed by the terms of reference and the procedure established, together with any code of conduct adopted. Those arrangements will have to be interpreted. Difficult cases will arise where those arrangements do not exist, have not been documented, are ambiguous or are in conflict with each other.

## 14.10   A duty to reach a final decision

An expert's instructions will often be to reach a final decision, and it should usually not be difficult to imply that obligation. If he does not do so, he may be in breach of his contract and liable to the parties in damages for the consequences. For two contrasting examples of where experts were alleged to have produced an inconclusive decision, see 13.7.7.

## 14.11   Tortious liability

### 14.11.1   Where there is no contractual relationship

An expert may have no contractual relationship with the parties, either directly, or indirectly through an appointing authority. The expert may be appointed by a third party, such as a company secretary instructing auditors to value shares, which is what happened in *Arenson v Casson Beckman Rutley & Co* [1975] 3 WLR 815. Arguably the company secretary was acting as agent for the shareholders. That kind of arrangement should present no problems, and Lord Salmon certainly thought it did not matter. He said, at 835C:

> We do not know whether the [auditors] were asked to make the valuation on behalf of the company (which presumably was interested in the value of its own shares) or on behalf of [the buying and selling shareholders], nor do we know whether the [auditors] charged any fee for this valuation, and, if so, to whom, or whether they made their valuation as part of their ordinary duties as the company's auditors. Nor do I think this matters because, since the decision of [the House of Lords] in *Hedley Byrne & Co v Heller & Partners Ltd* [1964] AC 465, it is clear that quite apart from any contractual obligation, the respondents must have owed a

duty to [both shareholders] to use reasonable skill and care in making their valuation.

This quotation is important for the study of experts' liability in tort, but does not provide authoritative guidance for *Hedley Byrne* liability today. This category of special relationship is now characterised more by the knowledge of the maker of the statement that the recipient will rely on it: see Lord Denning MR in *Ministry of Housing and Local Government v Sharp* [1970] 2 QB 223 at 268G, and 13.11.

Very careful examination is also now given, as in all negligence claims, of

(1) the foreseeability of the damage;
(2) the proximity of the parties; and
(3) whether it is just and reasonable in all the circumstances that the duty should exist: see Lord Oliver in *Caparo Industries plc v Dickman* [1990] 2 WLR 358 at 379B.

## 14.11.2   *Experts do owe tortious duties of care*

No reported case has even suggested that an expert in the range of circumstances discussed in this book owes no duty in tort to the parties to the contract under which the expert makes his determination. There are good reasons for that. As restated by Lord Oliver in *Caparo v Dickman* (cited at 14.11.1) at 383H–384B, the duty is as follows:

(1) the advice must be required for a purpose, whether particularly specified or generally described, which is made known, either actually or inferentially, to the adviser when the advice is given;
(2) the adviser knows, either actually or inferentially, that the advice will be communicated to the 'advisee', either specifically or as a member of an ascertainable class, in order that it should be used by the advisee for that purpose;
(3) it is known, either actually or inferentially, that the advice so communicated is likely to be acted upon by the advisee for that purpose without further inquiry; and
(4) it is so acted upon by the advisee to his detriment. The word 'advice' is used, although in *Caparo v Dickman* the 'advice' consisted of the audit of a company, which is more similar to an expert determination than advice given, for instance, by a lawyer.

From these criteria it should follow that an expert making a determination under a contract between two parties owes a duty of care to both those parties, because both will rely on him and him alone to get the determination right, if for no other reason than that they will be bound by it. However, the general rules of 'Hedley Byrne' type liability have to be borne in mind. The expert's liability in tort can never be more extensive than liability under any related contract, and whether the expert will be liable at all will always depend on the particular context and purpose of the particular statement.

### 14.11.3 'Triggers'

These criteria should exempt from liability an expert who issues a certificate under one contract which triggers events in another contract: for an example, see 7.4.4. An expert owes no duty in tort if there has been no reference of an issue to him and he did not know who would be affected by his certificate. (This applies only to the expert's tortious liability to the party with whom he has no contractual relationship: see 14.11.2.)

### 14.11.4 *Expert appointed by one party only*

The position where the expert is appointed by one party only is more doubtful. In *Panamena Europea Navigacion (Compania Limitada) v Frederick Leyland & Co Ltd (J Russell & Co)* [1947] AC 428 a surveyor was appointed by a ship's owners to certify the amount to be paid to ship repairers, and held to have acted as an expert (and as a 'quasi-arbitrator'). The surveyor would, if sued for negligence in 1947, have been immune.

### 14.11.5. *Limitation*

An expert's liability may run in both contract and tort, which may help a claimant where the limitation period is longer in tort: see Preston and Newsom's *Limitation of Actions*, 4th edn edited by John Weeks (Longman, 1989) at 3.4.

# Chapter 15

# Arbitration is Different

## 15.1 Summary

This chapter seeks to distinguish arbitration from references to experts by considering:
(1) confusion between whether references have been to experts or arbitrators (15.2);
(2) how the court interprets express words in the contract about a referee's status (15.3);
(3) the guidelines for assessing the referee's status (15.4–15.9);
(4) the procedural differences between arbitrations and references to experts (15.10);
(5) the different consequences of an expert's decision and an arbitration award (15.11).

## 15.2 Is the reference to an expert or an arbitrator?

### 15.2.1 A great controversy

This question has occupied the courts more than any other raised by the whole subject of expert determination. The question has been so controversial because of uncertainty about the law relating to arbitrators and experts generally and because of the differences between the consequences of an expert's decision and the consequences of an arbitration award. The differences between those consequences have themselves varied over the years: the current position is set out at 15.11.

### 15.2.2 Background from earlier chapters

Chapter 12 demonstrates that arbitration awards are easier to enforce than experts' decisions. Chapter 13 shows the limited potential for challenge to experts' decisions: this chapter summarises the current law on arbitration appeals, which has greatly restricted what was until 1979 very wide access indeed. Chapter 14 shows how experts have become liable for breach of duty, while arbitrators are immune.

### 15.2.3 Reasons for raising the controvesy

Arbitration is different. A dissatisfied party may want to establish that the reference was made to an expert so that he can then sue the individual, or that the reference was made to an arbitrator so that he can appeal against the award: or again there may be differences in rights of enforcement prompting the claim that an arbitration was a reference to an expert, or vice versa.

## 15.3 Express words

### 15.3.1 Considered with other evidence about the reference

The court will look at the words of the expert clause which, if unambiguous, may be significant evidence of the intentions of the parties about the procedure that eventuated. However, that evidence has to be considered along with what issue the referee had to consider and what actually happened in the reference.

### 15.3.2 Express words not conclusive ...

For instance, in *Taylor v Yielding* (1912) 56 SJ 253, Neville J said: 'The cases are quite clear that you cannot make a valuer an arbitrator by calling him so or vice versa'. The report is very brief, and the judge's full reasons are not set out: but it is a telling remark. The cases he relied on were mainly about references involving 'umpires' being valuations and not arbitrations. For instance, in *Re Hammond and Waterton* (1890) 62 LT 808, arbitrators were designated by the parties' agreement to assess the amount of compensation to be paid by an outgoing tenant of a market garden to his landlord. The judge said he believed the parties intended the reference to be a valuation, because of the appointment as the 'arbitrators' of a seedsman and a market gardener, both being, in his view, eminently suitable persons to assess the compensation by exercising their own skill and knowledge without any evidence or witnesses being called before them. Thus evidence of express words is not conclusive proof of the intentions of the parties.

### 15.3.3 ... but still very persuasive

However, the clearer the words used, the more difficult a contrary view becomes. In *Palacath Ltd v Flanagan* [1985] 2 All ER 161, the terms of a lease stated that the rent reviewer was to act as an expert and not as an arbitrator. The rent reviewer sought to defend an action for negligence on the basis that he was an arbitrator or quasi-arbitrator. Mars-Jones J agreed with the dictum in *Taylor v Yielding* (cited at 15.3.2) and said that the clause in the lease was not conclusive. But the judge did find the wording to be a very potent factor, and, after reviewing the guidelines discussed below, he found that the decision had indeed been that of an expert.

### 15.3.4 Is the wording ambiguous?

Where the wording of the expert clause is ambiguous, the court will look first at the other words in the document to resolve the ambiguity: see 8.17.3 and the decision summarised there in *Langham House Developments Ltd v Brompton Securities Ltd* (1980) 256 EG 719.

### 15.3.5 Confused drafting

Clauses are sometimes encountered which state that a referee is to be appointed who is described as an expert and then told that he will act as an arbitrator, or, alternatively, that the referee is an arbitrator who will act as an expert. The confusion created by this can be very wasteful. Apart from creating the excuse for a dispute about the procedure, it also perpetuates the misunderstanding of the differences between the two procedures: see 15.5.6.

## 15.4 Guidelines

### 15.4.1 Lord Wheatley's list

Where a reference, or part of one, has taken place, the courts consider a number of factors to establish whether the reference was to an expert or an arbitrator, and those factors have become known as 'indicia', because of the use of that word by Lord Wheatley in *Arenson v Casson Beckman Rutley & Co* [1975] 3 WLR 815. In this book the word 'guideline' is used in preference to the Latin. There are many cases on the distinction: *Arenson* is the starting-point for the modern law on the subject. In that case the defendant auditors claimed immunity from an action for negligence. Following the recent decision in *Sutcliffe v Thackrah* [1974] 1 AC 727, which had decided that a certifier under a building contract did not have arbitral immunity, the issue in *Arenson* was whether the defendants' valuation of shares was an arbitration. Lord Wheatley said (at p 830A-B) that although each case had to be decided on its own facts, there were four guidelines to assist in determining whether the valuer had the benefit of arbitral immunity. They were as follows:

(1) there is a dispute or a difference between the parties which has been formulated in some way or other (see 15.5);

(2) the dispute or difference has been remitted by the parties to the person to resolve in such a manner that he is called on to exercise a judicial function (see 15.6);

(3) where appropriate, the parties must have been provided with an opportunity to present evidence and/or submissions in support of their respective claims in the dispute (see 15.7); and

(4) the parties have agreed to accept his decision (see 15.8).

### 15.4.2 Guidelines—and therefore not conclusive

The following sections seek to evaluate these guidelines. As they are guidelines, none is conclusive on its own, and a combination of the guidelines may not be either. In a recent case, *Bridger Properties Ltd v Dovey Holdings (South Wales) Ltd* (1991) unreported, Chancery Division, 25 June: discussed at 7.4.4) the court did not consider the guidelines at all but simply observed that nothing could be more 'uncommercial' than to make the date for completion of a contract for sale and purchase of land turn upon the determination of an arbitrator.

## 15.5 A formulated dispute

### 15.5.1 The traditional distinction between experts and arbitrators

The notion that a 'formulated dispute' (ie an issue on which the parties have taken defined positions) is necessary to make the valuer or expert into an arbitrator is deep-rooted. In *Collins v Collins* (1856) 26 Beav 306 at 312, Sir John Romilly MR said:

... fixing the price of a property may be 'arbitration' ... but ... an arbitration is a reference to the decision of one or more persons ... of some matter ... in difference between the parties ... It is very true that in one sense it must be implied that although there is no existing difference, still that a difference may arise between the parties: yet I think the distinction between an existing difference and one which may arise is a material one, and one which has properly been relied on in this case ... It may well be that the decision of a particular valuer appointed might fix the price and might be equally satisfactory to both: so it can hardly be said there is a difference between them. Undoubtedly, as a general rule, the seller wants to get the highest price for his property, and the purchaser wishes to give the lowest, and in that sense it may be said that an expected difference between the parties is to be implied in every case, but unless a difference has actually arisen, it does not appear to me to be an 'arbitration'. Undoubtedly, if two persons enter into an arrangement for the sale of any particular property, and try to settle the terms, but cannot agree, and after dispute and discussion respecting the price, they say, 'We will refer this question of price to AB, he shall settle it', and thereupon they agree that the matter shall be referred to his arbitration, that would appear to be an 'arbitration', in the proper sense of the term...; but if they agree to a price to be fixed by another, that does not appear to me to be an arbitration.

### 15.5.2 Case with no dispute yet held to be an arbitration

In *Tharsis Sulphur & Copper Co Ltd v Loftus* (1872) LR 8 CP 1, the court (Bovill CJ during argument) found that the amount of an average adjustment was 'in question' between the parties under the terms of their agreement to refer, and therefore appears to have concluded that the reference to the average adjuster to apportion cargo damage was the reference of a dispute. However, as Lord Salmon said in *Sutcliffe v Thackrah* [1974] 1 AC 727 at 762C and D:

... there does not seem to have been any dispute between the parties [in *Tharsis Sulphur*]. They both knew that a loss had been suffered which had to be apportioned between them, but there is nothing to show that they had any idea, let alone conflicting ideas, of what the correct apportionment should be. Each of them might have engaged a separate average adjuster to advise him: had these not agreed, a dispute could have arisen between the parties which they might have submitted to arbitration—a somewhat unusual course in business of this kind. Instead, they sensibly decided to avoid disputes and differences by jointly employing one average adjuster to advise them on how the loss should be apportioned and agreed to accept and act on his advice.

### 15.5.3 An architect's certificate is not the decision of a dispute

In *Chambers v Goldthorpe* [1901] 1 QB 624, the Court of Appeal had to assert, at some length, that a formulated dispute was *not* necessary to give arbitral immunity to an architect certifying payments due to a contractor under a building contract. This issue was therefore of major importance for the House of Lords when they overruled *Chambers v Goldthorpe* in *Sutcliffe v Thackrah* (cited at 15.5.2). They held that the architect's giving of an interim certificate was not the decision of a dispute between the plaintiff and his builders and that there would need to be a dispute for the architect to qualify as an arbitrator: see Lord Reid at [1974] AC 737 H. (For a discussion of the difference between experts and certifiers in construction contracts, see 7.4.2.)

### 15.5.4   Auditors as arbitrators?

In *Leigh v English Pty Corporation Ltd* [1976] 2 Lloyd's Rep 298, a company's articles of association were silent as to whether its auditors should value its shares as experts or as arbitrators. The court said that because the articles showed that the auditors were not to be called in until the parties showed they were in disagreement, the auditors were to act as arbitrators. This raises the question of whether a partnership, such as a firm of accountants, or a corporation can act as arbitrators. Mustill and Boyd (p 247) state they cannot, but cite no authority. An arbitral tribunal is often composed of three or sometimes of five individuals, but all those individuals take a full part in the proceedings. Some modern firms of accountants number hundreds of partners, and their appointment as arbitrators would be inconsistent with the concept of all the members of a tribunal playing a full role by, for instance, attending the hearing. The decision on the existence of a dispute in *Leigh* therefore led the court into error over the capacity of a partnership to act as arbitrators.

### 15.5.5   A dispute can be referred to an expert

Scott J (as he then was) considered the question in *North Eastern Cooperative Society Ltd v Newcastle upon Tyne City Council* [1987] 1 EGLR 142, a case about ambiguous provisions in a lease about the status of the rent reviewer, and said at 146A:

> ... there was, of course, a dispute between the parties at the time in question in the sense that they could not agree on the amount of the yearly rent; but it was not a dispute in which each had formulated a view which was then placed for decision before the independent surveyor. The independent surveyor asked for their submissions in order to assist him in his task. He did not proceed on the footing that he was obliged to have their submissions.

This passage contains the important concession that the existence of a dispute does not preclude a reference to an expert.

Scott J said that the distinction lay in whether the parties would have been prepared to allow the matter to be decided on the basis of views which had not been formulated.

### 15.5.6 Ipswich v Fisons

The guideline of whether a dispute has been formulated between the parties has recently been restated in *Ipswich Borough Council v Fisons plc* [1990] 1 WLR 108. The headnote in the Weekly Law Reports is wrong: it states that the lease provided that disputes were to be referred to arbitration, whereas in fact the lease between Ipswich and Fisons said that if Fisons did not accept Ipswich's terms the matter should be referred to an *independent expert*. The serious consequences of confusion between experts and arbitrators are underlined by the fact that the subject-matter of this case that the Court of Appeal had to deal with was nothing more than the rent of a car park. Purporting to act under the terms of the lease, the parties appointed an arbitrator, and Ipswich appealed against his award. The case is important for establishing the circumstances in which the courts will allow an appeal from an arbitration award. It is important for expert determination because of the words of Lord Donaldson MR, who said at 115D:

[The expert] was not determining the rights and obligations of the parties. They were not in dispute. He was fixing the terms in the exercise of his professional skill and judgment ... Undoubtedly the parties did not see it like this. They seem to have concluded that the *independent expert would be acting as an arbitrator* ... (emphasis added).

This goes to the heart of how some judges would like to define the essential difference between experts and arbitrators. The curious facts of *Ipswich v Fisons* were being relied on to support the distinction. Lord Donaldson was suggesting that the parties made an informed decision that the matter had to be referred to arbitration on the basis that they had a formulated dispute where their rights and obligations were to be determined. Probably in this case (as in many others) the parties and their lawyers were not familiar with the distinction and were just confused, and may not even have realised that there is a distinction.

### 15.5.7 *Transition to the next guideline*

Commenting on this guideline in *Capricorn Inks Pty Ltd v Lawter International (Australasia) Pty Ltd* [1989] 1 Qd R 8, at 15, McPherson J said:

... the existence of a 'dispute', although a factor, is not necessarily a decisive factor in determining whether arbitration or appraisement is involved. It is quite possible for parties to become involved in a dispute about something, such as the value of premises or goods, which they agree to submit for appraisal without intending that an arbitration should follow. The distinction depends on a range of factors of varying importance and weight depending on the circumstances; but generally what must be in contemplation is that there will be 'an inquiry in the nature of a judicial inquiry' (quoted from Lord Esher MR in *Re Carus-Wilson and Greene* (1886) 18 QBD 7, at 9).

This leads to the next guideline.

## 15.6   A judicial function

### 15.6.1   A judge is not an expert

To be an arbitrator, the referee will have to be shown, in deciding the matter between the parties, to have exercised the functions of a judge. It is not the function of a judge to use his own expertise in a given area outside the law and the administration of justice. This rule has recently been restated: in *R v Simbodyal* (1991) *The Times*, 10 October, the Court of Appeal criticised a judge for having

turned himself into a handwriting expert and compared examples of the defendant's signature ... A judge should not be seen as a witness who held himself capable of comparing handwriting and reached conclusions of the comparisons.

This was a criminal case, but the principle is the same in civil cases.

This guideline often overlaps with the next one, which relates to the manner in which judicial inquiries are conducted, with particular reference to evidence and submissions.

### 15.6.2   Re Hopper

The line of authority starts with *Re Hopper* (1867) LR 2 QB 367, which was about the assessment of compensation payable by a tenant farmer. The court took the view that the case raised issues that were sufficiently difficult, as could be seen from the fact that the parties were represented at the hearing by counsel, to justify the decision that the procedure had been an arbitration. In *Sutcliffe v Thackrah* [1974] AC 727 at 763D Lord Salmon explained the point as follows:

In *Re Hopper* Cockburn CJ ... was ... saying that the question whether anyone was to be treated as an arbitrator depended on whether the role which he performed was invested with the characteristic attributes of the judicial role. If an expert were employed to certify, make a valuation or appraisal or settle compensation as between opposing interests, this did not, of itself, put him in the position of an arbitrator. He might ... do no more than examine goods or work or accounts and make a decision accordingly. On the other hand, he might, as in *Re Hopper*, hear the evidence and submissions of the parties, in which case he would clearly be regarded as an arbitrator ...

### 15.6.3  Arbitrators using their own expertise

Where arbitrators have behaved more like experts and relied on their own expertise, their awards have been set aside. In *Annie Fox v P G Wellfair Ltd (in liquidation)* and *Philip Fisher v P G Wellfair Ltd (in liquidation)* [1981] 2 Lloyd's Rep 514, the respondents did not take part in the proceedings but the applicants produced expert evidence at the hearing. The court said that the conclusion the arbitrator had come to could only have been reached by in effect giving evidence to himself in flat contradiction to the evidence given by the applicants' expert witness, and the arbitrator was guilty of misconduct in failing to observe the rules of natural justice. In *Top Shop Estates v Danino, Same v Tandy Corporation* [1985] 1 EGLR 9, a surveyor conducted a rent review of a shop as an arbitrator. Without telling the parties, he collected a series of pedestrian counts which he considered relevant. His award was also set aside, Leggatt J remarking that the arbitrator's function was not to play the part of Perry Mason where he felt that the submissions or evidence of the parties might usefully be supplemented. However, a rent review arbitrator was allowed rather more latitude in disagreeing with the expert witnesses of both parties in his assessment of valuation criteria in *Lex Services plc v Oriel House BV, Oriel House BV v Lex Services plc* [1991] 39 EG 139.

These problems do not arise if the referee is an expert.

### 15.6.4  The 'ultimate test'

The 'ultimate test' was said by Mars-Jones J in *Palacath Ltd v Flanagan* [1985] 2 All ER 161, at p 166 to be:

... how is he [the referee] to arrive at his decision? Was he obliged to act wholly or in part on the evidence and submissions made by the parties? Or was he entitled to act solely on his own expert opinion? If the answer to the question is the latter, then the [referee] could not be exercising a judicial function or a quasi-judicial function, if there is any such distinction.

### 15.6.5  Commodity arbitrations

Some commodity arbitrations relating to quality and price seem to be in a separate category in this respect. By 'commodity arbitrations' are meant arbitrations conducted and administered under the rules of commodity trade associations in the City of London. For an account, see Derek Kirby Johnson in Part 4 of Ronald Bernstein's *Handbook of Arbitration Practice*. Many of these arbitrations are about the quality and/or condition of commodities like rice or coffee. The arbitrator's task is to look at and sniff the sample of the commodity and to apply his trade experience to determine its quality or condition. Kirby Johnson writes (47.1) on how cocoa beans would be assessed:

[The arbitrators] open the sample and cut the beans with a penknife and examine the interior for 'slateyness' and mould or other defects ... On the results of their cutting, [the arbitrators] agree whether an allowance [reducing the price] should be given, and if so, how much. This is entirely a matter of their personal skill and judgment.

### 15.6.6  A recognised categorisation

These arbitrators are experts in the non-legal sense of the word, and they do not perform a judicial function. But the categorisation of this procedure as arbitration is traditional and deeply rooted, and unlikely to take notice of the guidelines. In any case, the courts recognise the practice. For instance, in *Finnegan v Allen* [1943] 1 KB 425, at p436, Goddard LJ (as he then was) said:

The person appointed will be an expert in the trade who will look at the sample ... This is constantly done in Mincing Lane [a street in the City of London], and the person who acts in this way is, perhaps, a quasi-arbitrator or even an arbitrator, but he is an arbitrator of a particular sort, and it is not intended that there should be the same judicial proceeding on his part as there would be in the case of an arbitrator appointed under a formal submission.

This judge saw valuers/experts as quasi-arbitrators because he believed they should not be sued. He addressed the question again in *Mediterranean and Eastern Export Co Ltd v Fortress Fabrics (Manchester) Ltd* [1948] 2 All ER 186. The issue here was whether a chamber of commerce textile arbitration should have heard expert evidence. In this judgment there is no mention of 'quasi-arbitrators': it is fully accepted that the question of the quality of the textile was determined by an arbitrator acting on his own knowledge and experience.

### 15.6.7 Courts support arbitration rules

'Look/sniff' arbitrations, as these arbitrations have become known, have to be seen as an exception to this important guideline. The courts have not tried to change commercial practice in this respect. Rather, the courts have upheld commercial contracts incorporating the rules of commodity associations. Those rules specifically say that the arbitration is going to be conducted in this way.

### 15.6.8 The most important guideline?

With the important exception of look/sniff arbitrations, this guideline of a judicial function is probably the most important.

## 15.7 Evidence and submissions

### 15.7.1 Presentation an essential feature of an arbitration

The presentation, where appropriate, to the referee of evidence and submissions in support of their respective claims in the dispute was Lord Wheatley's third guideline. He said that if evidence and submissions are not present the procedure 'cannot' be an arbitration. This guideline has not attracted as much comment as the previous two, and has sometimes been seen as part of the second one.

### 15.7.2 An exception to this principle

In *Re Hopper* (1867) LR 2 QB 367, Lord Cockburn CJ said that a judicial inquiry was conducted on the principle of hearing the parties and the evidence of their witnesses. However, in *Bottomley v Ambler* (1878) 38 LT 545 an arbitration award was allowed to stand although the principle had not been followed. An umpire was appointed to determine the rent of a mill. The umpire gave no notice to the parties or their solicitors, examined no witnesses, but merely heard the statement of the two 'arbitrators' and inspected the premises. In his award he said that he had heard, examined, and considered the allegations, witnesses and evidence of all the parties. The Court of Appeal held that there was no ground for disturbing the award as the arbitrators and the umpire were all 'experts' and it was evidently the intention of the parties that they should settle the value and not act as formal arbitrators. Thesiger LJ said that arbitrators incurred 'enormous' expense in calling witnesses, 'which was entirely thrown away, for as soon as the arbitrators saw the property they knew at once what ought to be done'.

### 15.7.3  How do arbitrators and experts stand in relation to this guideline?

The presentation of submissions and evidence at a formal hearing (with witnesses available to be cross-examined) is a universal characteristic of litigation in England. The questions remain whether an arbitrator is obliged to follow the litigation practice and whether an expert is prohibited from doing so. The answers seem to be that:

(1) an arbitrator may be obliged to follow the litigation practice if he is to avoid an allegation of misconduct, unless the arbitration rules concerned specifically preclude those procedures or the parties both agree they need not be followed; and that

(2) the position of an expert will depend first on whether the parties have any specific requirements. Subject to that, an expert is not prohibited from following these litigation-style procedures, but he would be unwise to do so because the reference may subsequently be held to have been an arbitration and will in any event take longer and be more costly.

### 15.7.4  Two modern exceptions

The qualifying words 'where appropriate' in Lord Wheatley's phrase (quoted at 15.4.1(3) above) may point to certain types of arbitrations where evidence and submissions are not heard. These are the 'look/sniff' arbitrations discussed above (15.6.5) and 'documents-only' arbitrations discussed below (15.7.6). It may be helpful to consider an example of each.

### 15.7.5  Commodity arbitrations

From the description of the cocoa arbitration above (15.6.5), it is immediately apparent that there are no submissions or evidence. It is difficult to see what use submissions or evidence would be. Presumably each side would want to state its position about the quality/condition of the sample and the evidence would presumably be about other samples said to be of various qualities or conditions. But the arbitrator is sufficiently expert to enable him to decide just by inspection of the goods in dispute.

### 15.7.6 'Documents-only' arbitrations

'Documents-only' arbitrations are procedures where the issues are decided on the basis of written submissions only, and there is no oral presentation of submissions or evidence. Documents-only arbitrations have been set up to provide a simple means of resolving complaints by consumers in a number of industries, such as travel and telephones. Arbitration is written into the standard form contracts as the form of dispute resolution to be used. Thus, if the consumer is dissatisfied with certain types of consumer service covered by one of these schemes, he has to refer the matter to a documents-only arbitration. Now, under the Consumer Arbitration Agreements Act 1988, the consumer has the choice between arbitration and the County Court, and the statute overrules the compulsory arbitration clause.

### 15.7.7 Procedure in 'documents-only' arbitrations

The procedure for 'documents-only' arbitrations is described by Margaret Rutherford in Part 5 of Ronald Bernstein's *Handbook of Arbitration Practice*. There is no formal hearing and no oral evidence: the documents consist of an application form, a claim form and a defence, each accompanied by copies of relevant documents such as the contract and correspondence, and the claimant's comments on the defence: it is on the basis of those documents that the arbitrator then makes his award: see Rutherford at 53.1. The documents-only procedure is also used in property valuation disputes and rent reviews: see W G Nutley in Part 8 of Ronald Bernstein's *Handbook of Arbitration Practice*. The procedure in 'documents-only' arbitrations is difficult to distinguish from the procedure in some references to an expert.

### 15.7.8 These exceptions resemble expert determination

Look/sniff arbitrations bear a strong resemblance to expert determinations, and documents-only arbitrations to determinations of general disputes by an expert (see 6.9). But they are arbitrations which contractually-incorporated rules and commercial practice make exempt from the requirement of submissions and oral evidence.

## 15.8    Agreement to accept the decision

### 15.8.1    An expert's decision is usually final and binding

Lord Wheatley's fourth and last guideline was that the parties had agreed to accept the referee's decision. This is often found in expert clauses (see 8.8), which state that the decision of the expert will be final and binding: see 6.8 for the important exceptions to that principle.

### 15.8.2    Arbitration appeals used to be commonplace

The essential difference here is that an arbitration award is subject to appeal to or review by the High Court. In the past this right was frequently exercised under what was known as the 'case stated' procedure. Hence, in *Baber v Kenwood Manufacturing Co Ltd and Whinney Murray* [1978] 1 Lloyd's Rep 175, Megaw LJ could say, at 179:

Why do the parties provide that the auditors 'shall be considered to be acting as experts and not as arbitrators'? For the simple reason that, if they were to be considered as arbitrators, there would be at least a danger that one party or the other might be able to require a case to be stated before a court of law, by which means it could be suggested that the award was not binding because of some error in it.

### 15.8.3    Abolition of 'case stated' procedure

The very next year, the Arbitration Act 1979 abolished the 'case stated' procedure (s 1(1)) and introduced the right to exclude appeals altogether in certain cases. In domestic cases appeals can be excluded only after the dispute has arisen (s 3(6)), and in both domestic and international disputes appeals cannot be excluded in admiralty, commodity and insurance cases (s 4(1)). However, in all other international cases the procedures can be excluded at the time of making the original contract (s 3(1)). Since 1979 the courts have ruled that review and appeal are available only where certain standard forms of contract need to be interpreted by the court or an award is plainly and seriously wrong: see Jaffe in (1989) *Arbitration* vol 55, p 184. The general effect is that opportunities for review and appeal are very limited in arbitrations. However, the court can also still remit or set aside an arbitration award, under s 22 and s 23 of the Arbitration Act 1950, and this continues to be a relatively frequently exercised right. The counterpart for expert determination is the line taken by the courts in the recent cases of *Jones v Sherwood Computer Services plc* [1991] NPC 60 and *Nikko Hotels (UK) Ltd v MEPC Ltd*

[1991] 28 EG 86: see 13.6. There is no machinery for remission for misconduct in expert determination.

### 15.8.4 The courts uphold agreed procedures

To summarise, the court's policy is strongly in favour of upholding contractual dispute procedures, and against allowing access to the courts where contractually agreed disputes procedures alternative to the court have not failed: see 13.14.4.

## 15.9 Review of the guidelines

### 15.9.1 The guidelines are not conclusive

From the above it is reasonably clear that:
(1) the question of whether there is a 'formulated dispute' is not conclusive;
(2) the requirements of a judicial function and the judicial procedures of submissions and evidence are conclusive unless specifically contradicted by commercial practice and/or contractually incorporated rules; and
(3) the agreement to accept the decision is not conclusive.

*Russell on Arbitration* (20th edn, p 54) states:

It is seldom an easy matter to determine in any given case whether the parties intended an arbitration or a valuation. Every fact and circumstance must be considered and it will probably be seldom that any single one is determinative.

### 15.9.2 A third category?

The courts may find it impossible to categorise every procedure it is asked to review as either a reference to an expert or an arbitrator. In *Re Carus-Wilson & Greene* (1886) 18 QBD 7 at 9, Lord Esher MR said:

There may be cases of an intermediate kind, where, though a person is appointed to settle disputes that have arisen, still it is not intended that he shall be bound to hear evidence and arguments. In such cases it may be often difficult to say whether he is intended to be an arbitrator or to exercise some function other than that of an arbitrator.

Maybe it is into this category that one should place the borderline cases identified above (15.7.7), particularly the reference to experts of general disputes (6.9). In the current judicial climate, difficulties in categorisation should not make a decision or award in contention any more likely to be upset.

### 15.9.3 Diminishing importance of the controversy

The changes in arbitration law may make this question less important in the future; a finding that a reference was an arbitration will not improve the chances of a successful challenge, because the opportunities for appeals from arbitration awards are now so scarce: see 15.8.3. The issue will, however, continue to be important for negligence claims where the defendant wishes to seek immunity on the grounds that he acted as an arbitrator, as in *Palacath Ltd v Flanagan* [1985] 2 All ER 161: see 14.5.3.

## 15.10 Procedural differences

### 15.10.1 Expert procedure depends on contract

Chapter 11 discussed the procedure for expert determination. There is no official model and the procedure for any given reference depends on the expert clause in the original contract between the parties and subsequent directions by the expert. The parties' rights in the resulting procedure are established by the law of contract.

### 15.10.2 Arbitration procedure is moving away from litigation

Arbitration is used in a wide range of disputes, and procedures can be tailored to suit the occasion, although practitioners are understandably cautious, given the serious consequences of an allegation of misconduct. The reform of arbitration procedure is a controversial subject, with many wishing to detach arbitration from close adherence to litigation procedures. This trend is marked by s 103 of the Courts and Legal Services Act 1990, which has abolished the court's power to enforce an arbitrator's order for interrogatories and discovery of documents. Interrogatories are questions put by one party to the other about his case which that other party must answer: discovery is a process by which both parties must disclose to each other all documents relevant to the issues, except for documents containing legal advice on the case. The trend away from litigation procedures may continue: perhaps Parliament might also abolish the right to subpoena witnesses to attend arbitrations, a right which survives in s 12(4) of the Arbitration Act 1950.

### 15.10.3  Insisting on a hearing

Parties to an arbitration can agree to dispense with a hearing, but if they do not, one party can insist on a hearing: Mustill and Boyd, pp 300–301.

### 15.10.4  'Misconduct'

Section 22 and s 23 of the Arbitration Act 1950 preserve the right to apply to the court to set aside an award on the ground of misconduct by the arbitrator: misconduct sometimes amounts to what appear to be no more than minor procedural solecisms. The right to seek remission or removal for misconduct is a statutory remedy in arbitration law with no real common law analogue in expert determination.

### 15.10.5  Two types of arbitration more like expert determination

The procedure in 'look/sniff' and 'documents-only' arbitrations is very close to that of expert determination: see 15.7.8.

### 15.10.6  Tactics

The differences in procedure between expert determination and arbitration may be only potential in some cases. But any one of those differences can be very important tactically where one party is prepared to exploit the opportunity. Allegations of misconduct by the arbitrator are an obvious example of a tactic available in arbitration and not in expert determination: 15.10.4. The parties' legal costs are recoverable in arbitrations but not in expert determinations, unless specific provision is made: see 8.13. Tactics are discussed further in Chapter 16.

## 15.11  The different consequences of an expert's decision and an arbitration award

### 15.11.1  General

Parties faced with an expert's decision or an arbitration award will need to know how the decision or award may be enforced, whether they can appeal against the decision or award and whether they can sue the expert or arbitrator.

### 15.11.2  Enforcement

An expert's decision cannot be enforced by the courts without issuing a writ and obtaining judgment, and it is not enforceable internationally without court proceedings in at least one country.

An arbitration award can be enforced by a simple procedure, and is enforceable internationally. See further Chapter 12.

### 15.11.3 Appeals from experts' decisions

A party who wishes to appeal from a decision of an expert will be able to do so only:
(1) if the expert has decided the wrong issue; or
(2) if the expert has asked himself the wrong question: see 13.6.8.

An expert misconducts himself only if he fails to decide the issue in the way he has agreed with the parties to do: see 13.13.

### 15.11.4 Appeals from arbitration awards

A party who wishes to appeal from an arbitration award will be able to do so only:
(1) if he has not entered into an international contract where the right to appeal has been excluded; or
(2) if he has not agreed to exclude the right to appeal after the dispute has arisen; or
(3) if the subject-matter is admiralty, commodities or insurance; or
(4) if he is challenging a finding where there is a need to interpret certain standard form contracts; or
(5) if he is challenging a finding which is plainly and seriously wrong.

A dissatisfied party may also consider an allegation of misconduct against the arbitrator. See further 15.8.3 and 15.10.4.

### 15.11.5 Suing experts and arbitrators

A party who wishes to sue an expert will have to prove professional negligence or some other breach of contract. An arbitrator is immune from suit, both by statute and at common law. See further 14.7.

# Chapter 16

# Tactics

## 16.1 Summary

This chapter:
(1) considers tactics in negotiating agreements (16.2);
(2) lists and considers the factors which influence the choice of disputes procedure (16.3);
(3) reviews tactics after a dispute has arisen (16.4) and during a reference (16.5); and
(4) assesses the place of expert determination in the context of alternative dispute resolution (16.6).

## 16.2 Negotiating agreements

### 16.2.1 Choice of applications

At the negotiating stage parties can choose a number of possible applications for the expert clause. The traditional valuation /technical expertise function is available for ascertaining future valuations or resolving technical disputes; and it is now more likely to be suggested for resolving general, non-technical disputes as well.

### 16.2.2 Expert determination not used in banking agreements

The summary jurisdiction of the High Court under RSC Ord 14 is the best way to obtain a final judgment in a matter of default. It is therefore not surprising that neither expert determination nor arbitration have found a place in banking documents like loan agreements, where the bank will wish to be able to enforce its rights against the borrower as quickly and effectively as possible. No matters of valuation or expertise arise.

### 16.2.3 Questionable advisability of general dispute resolution

The advisability of general dispute resolution by experts is at the present more questionable, because, as has been seen (6.9), the results can be unacceptable and the method sufficiently unusual to encourage challenges. However, it is likely that this method will gain ground: for the consequences, see 17.5. As can be seen later in this chapter, the search is on for simpler and cheaper forms of dispute resolution.

### 16.2.4   Too easy an option?

Perceptions and bargaining strengths play their part. There has recently been a trend away from expert clauses in tax liability clauses in sale and purchase agreements; apparently it is believed that parties are more likely to reach agreement amongst themselves if they know that the consequences of an unresolved dispute are court proceedings, and reference to an expert is seen as too easy an option and one that does not encourage agreement.

### 16.2.5   The agent of one party only

Sometimes one of the parties may express a stronger bargaining position by insisting on a clause giving its agent such as its auditors, the right to determine an issue: see 7.4.3 for the sparse authority.

### 16.2.6   One of the parties acting as expert?

What happens if the agreement provides that one of the parties should itself determine the issue? A clause of this type was upheld in *Bache & Co (London) Ltd v Banque Vernes et Commerciale de Paris SA* [1973] 2 Lloyd's Rep 437. For a telling criticism of the judgment see the article by Lawrence Collins and Dorothy Livingston cited in Further Reading.

These are some of the tactical considerations. The question of tactics is pursued further in the next section which provides a comparison of expert determination with arbitration and litigation.

## 16.3   Factors influencing choice of disputes procedure

### 16.3.1   Speed

A properly conducted reference to an expert should take less time than an arbitration or court case. The fact that expert references sometimes do take a long time usually results from using the wrong procedure and/or from delays caused by construction summonses.

## 16.3.2 Cost

As cost is so much a function of time, the cost of litigation and arbitration will generally be considerably higher than the cost of expert references. The following considerations also apply:

(1) There is no statutory control over experts' fees, whereas there is over the fees of arbitrators: see 14.2.4. In litigation, the costs of judges are borne by the state and not charged to the parties. Expert clauses usually say that the expert's fees are to be shared equally between the parties, irrespective of the result, but other variations are found: see 8.12.

(2) The expert cannot order one party to pay the other's costs unless the power is specifically stipulated: see 8.13.

(3) The proportion of irrecoverable costs in litigation and arbitration is a constant factor at about 35 per cent, to be weighed against the potential damages and the costs that are recoverable.

## 16.3.3 Procedure

Is a formal, adversarial procedure appropriate for dealing with the issues? If formality is required, litigation is indicated: but in any arbitration a formal hearing can be insisted on by one of the parties: see 15.10.3. Formal hearings are generally avoided in expert determinations: see 11.6.1. Witnesses can be subpoenaed to attend arbitration (see 15.10.2) and court hearings, but there is no such right in expert determination. Litigation obliges both parties to disclose all their documents to each other, and a similar process may be sought in arbitration, although it cannot now be enforced (see 15.10.2); general disclosure obligations do not suit expert determinations: see 11.6.4.

## 16.3.4 Legal questions

Legal questions can be argued between lawyers before a judge who can decide them: an arbitrator may hear submissions, but may not be qualified to decide on them and may seek outside help or recommend a reference to the court under s2 of the Arbitration Act 1979: an expert can take outside help, but not from the court.

## 16.3.5 Finality

The position used to be that if the parties wanted one final decision, even if it were wrong, they should choose the expert procedure, because it is difficult to challenge experts' decisions.

However, appeals from arbitration awards have recently become unavailable for most purposes (see 15.8.3), and there is little now in the point. Litigation provides appeals as of right.

### 16.3.6  Recourse

It is possible, however, difficult, to sue an expert for breach of duty (see Chapter 14): it is not possible to take similar action against an arbitrator or judge.

### 16.3.7  Privacy

References to experts and arbitrations are both private, whereas litigation is not. However, arbitration can lose its privacy by applications to the court, and by discovery obligations: *Shearson Lehman Hutton Incorporated v Maclaine Watson and Co Ltd* [1988] 1 WLR 946. There is a much narrower range of opportunities for applications to the court about expert determination. Special measures to ensure confidentiality between the parties can be taken in expert references (see 11.5.1): measures of that sort are rare in arbitration and unavailable in litigation.

### 16.3.8  Nature of likely disputes

(1) Some disputes have been traditionally referred to experts, and additions are still being made to the list. A procedure that has been used before will gain acceptance for its use again: where it is a new application, there will be more work for the draftsman. Arbitration is traditionally used for certain commodity disputes: see 6.2.1.

(2) Arbitration and litigation can be used for any kind of dispute, but those involving valuation or expertise are settled more efficiently by expert determination. Will it be a simple matter to avoid jurisdiction arguments about new claims of the type discussed in 16.5.3 ? If not, litigation is preferable to both arbitration and expert determination.

(3) On the use of expert determination for all disputes arising under a contract, both technical and general, see 6.9.

### 16.3.9  Relationship of the parties

Is there a continuing relationship worth saving? Expert determination should be a less hostile way of settling disputes than arbitration or litigation, particularly where there is to be a long-term contract. Aggressive litigation procedures which are often used in arbitration as well as litigation are not available in expert determination.

### 16.3.10   Location of the parties

International enforcement of experts' decisions can be difficult, whereas means to enforce judgments and arbitration awards internationally do exist: see 12.6.

## 16.4   Proposing expert determination after a dispute has arisen

### 16.4.1   The original choice of forum is part of the negotiations

The same check-list for choosing between means of dispute resolution will apply after a dispute has arisen. But there will be an additional factor. The parties' contract will provide a means of dispute resolution. Either a specific means of dispute resolution will have been chosen, or court litigation will be implied where no particular choice has been made. Both parties will wish to obtain the best advantage from whatever means they have to use. Thus a badly drafted expert clause (or a badly drafted arbitration clause) may give a considerable advantage to a party wishing to postpone proceedings and avoid liability.

### 16.4.2   A sign of weakness?

Where a dispute has arisen over a contract which does not contain an expert clause and one party proposes expert determination, the other party may see it as a sign of weakness because it signals an unwillingness and an inability to pursue the case through the courts or arbitration. The other party is likely to maintain this view unless he believes that it will be to his ultimate disadvantage to insist on the dispute being litigated or arbitrated, where the costs risk cannot be justified: see 16.3.2.

## 16.5   Conducting a reference

### 16.5.1   Disputes arising from poor drafting

The tactics in conducting a reference will depend on the presence and significance of difficulties raised by poor drafting of the expert clause, where the parties have not seen it in their interests to deal with these problems or taken the opportunity to clarify the points of difficulty in terms of reference.

## 16.5.2 *Poorly defined issues*

Poor definition of the issue to be determined can be a particular problem. It will lead either to delay, or confusion, or both. Delay may be caused by a construction summons where one party applies to the court to clarify the ambiguity in the definition of the issue. If that route is not followed, there may be continuing confusion over what the issue really is, which may have a number of adverse consequences, including the expert's failure to arrive at a decision on the right issue.

## 16.5.3 *Jurisdiction arguments*

But there are dangers in defining the issue too closely. Attempts to enlarge the scope of a reference may be resisted with arguments about jurisdiction familiar to arbitration practitioners (see Mustill and Boyd, p 125). Briefly, the problem is that a party who wishes to restrict the scope of the dispute, or who simply finds it serves his interests to be awkward, can prevent associated claims being heard in the same reference, which obliges the other party to initiate a second reference.

An awkward party may have opportunities for exploiting instances of poor drafting of any other parts of the expert clause, the terms of reference or procedural directions.

## 16.6 Alternative dispute resolution

### 16.6.1 *American origins*

Alternative dispute resolution, or ADR as it is often known, is any means of resolving disputes which is alternative to the court procedure. It has been particularly prominent in the United States, where the courts offer commercial litigants years of expensive preparation culminating in a jury trial with unpredictable and sometimes very alarming results. Forms of arbitration have therefore become more popular in the United States, as arbitration is and always has been seen as a form of alternative dispute resolution. Many other forms have also been tried. They are all based on mediation or conciliation. The most famous is the 'mini-trial', publicised by the Center for Public Resources in New York. The 'mini-trial' is a combination of presentation and negotiation presided over by a 'neutral'. These procedures are said to have the advantage of saving time and money, particularly legal fees, and enabling parties to continue a friendly commercial relationship.

However, the way mini-trials are conducted is bound to produce some unjust results, and they may produce no result at all, as no-one can be forced to negotiate a settlement.

### 16.6.2  Slow development in England

Recent years have seen a great deal of interest in Europe about alternative dispute resolution, which has been part of the trend away from litigation-type procedures in arbitration (15.10.2). There have been many articles about ADR, both in the legal journals and the national press, and videos about ADR have been made and shown at conferences. However, very little practical ADR has actually taken place this side of the Atlantic: or, if it has, no-one has given it publicity. But the interest continues to be strong, and a number of organisations are promoting ADR in England, notably The Centre for Dispute Resolution, CEDR.

### 16.6.3  Expert determination is binding, ADR is not

Against that background the development of expert determination may well be given further impetus. The essential difference between it and all other forms of ADR is that expert determination does produce a result which is binding on the parties, whereas ADR does not.

# Chapter 17

# Public Policy

## 17.1  Summary

This chapter:
(1) shows that the law gives effect to contracts which are technically valid unless they offend some principle of public policy (17.2);
(2) shows that upholding experts' decisions does not offend any principle of public policy, because the court's jurisdiction is not completely ousted (17.3);
(3) makes comparisons with other determinations by third parties (17.4); and
(4) concludes with an assessment of the combined effect of experts deciding general, non-technical disputes and the courts denying challenges to decisions (17.5).

## 17.2  The law should give effect to contracts

### 17.2.1  Primacy of contract law

Earlier chapters have shown, again and again, that references to experts are contracts enforced as contracts according to the law of contract.

### 17.2.2  Judicial examples

In *Photo Production Ltd v Securicor Transport Ltd* [1980] AC 827, Lord Diplock said, at 848: 'A basic principle of [contract law] is that the parties are free to determine for themselves what primary obligations they will accept'. In that case, an exclusion clause allowed Securicor to escape all liability for the burning down of a factory, which had been caused by their employee's negligence. Another graphic reminder of this policy is to be found in *Temloc v Errill Properties Ltd* (1989) 39 BLR 30, where the

148

Court of Appeal refused to allow the owner any claim for damages in a building contract where the word 'nil' had been written in as the amount of liquidated damages: the choice of liquidated damages precluded a claim for damages at large, and the writing in of nil was said (by Nourse LJ at 39) to be 'an exhaustive agreement as to damages. . . payable by the contractor in the event of his failure to complete the works on time'.

The natural corollary of being able to make whatever contract you like is that the court will enforce whatever contract is made. If a contract is technically valid, the only reason for not enforcing it is that to do so would offend some principle of public policy.

## 17.3 No contrary reason of public policy

### 17.3.1 The principle of 'ouster'

The public policy objection to upholding experts' decisions would be that the procedure 'ousts' the jurisdiction of the court. The principle of 'ouster' is that no provision purporting to exclude a right to sue in court will be recognised: *Doleman and sons v Osset Corporation* [1912] 3 KB 257. Its arbitration context is explained in Mustill and Boyd (p 57): the court has the right to intervene both to safeguard its own procedures and to invalidate agreed procedures if they are contrary to fundamental principles.

### 17.3.2 Scott v Avery *clauses*

All arbitration clauses by definition result in the court's jurisdiction being ousted to some extent. The *'Scott v Avery'* type of arbitration clause (named after the case of *Scott v Avery* (1855) 5 HLC 809) states that an arbitration award is a condition precedent to the enforcement of rights under the contract. If one of the parties starts court proceedings, the clause does not invalidate the action, but provides a defence and postpones enforcement: see Mustill and Boyd, p 162. Presumably a similar provision making expert determination a condition precedent to the enforcement of rights under a contract would be upheld by the courts in the same way.

### 17.3.3 An attempt to exclude appeals by contract

In *Czarnikow v Roth, Schmidt & Co* [1922] 2 KB 478, the Court of Appeal decided that the then current arbitration rules of the Refined Sugar Association were an ouster of the court's jurisdiction, in that they prevented applications to the court under the 'case stated' procedure. Section 1(1) of the Arbitration Act 1979 abolished the 'case stated' procedure and s 3 permitted parties to agree in certain cases to exclude all rights of appeal. Parliament is sovereign and decides when the jurisdiction of the court can be ousted.

### 17.3.4   Ouster must be total

On the same basis as arbitration, a reference to an expert does not oust the jurisdiction of the court, as the court has jurisdiction over the conduct of the reference, the decision and its enforcement. In exercising its jurisdiction the court applies only the law of contract, and although the court does not intervene on any other ground, the effect is that the court's jurisdiction is not ousted; although the ouster is substantial, it is not complete, and not sufficient to be contrary to public policy.

### 17.3.5   Questions of law

The issue of whether questions of law have a special status was considered in *Nikko Hotels (UK) Ltd v MEPC plc* [1991] 28 EG 86. The judge said that Lord Wright's remarks in *F R Absalom Ltd v Great Western (London) Garden Village Society* [1933] AC 592 at 615 showed that there was no rule of public policy preventing parties from agreeing to remit a question of law to the exclusive and final jurisdiction of an expert. This contradicts the view taken by Denning LJ (as he then was) in *Lee v Showmen's Guild of Great Britain* [1952] 2 QB 329 at 342:

Although the jurisdiction of a domestic tribunal is founded on the contract ... the parties are not free to make any contract they like. There are important limitations imposed by public policy ... They can ... agree to leave questions of law, as well as questions of fact, to the decision of the domestic tribunal. They can, indeed, make the tribunal the final arbiter on questions of fact, but they cannot make it the final arbiter on questions of law. They cannot prevent its decisions being examined by the courts. If the parties should seek, by agreement, to take the law out of the hands of the courts and put it into the hands of a private tribunal, without any recourse at all to the courts in the case of an error of law, then the agreement is to that extent contrary to public policy and void: ... (citing *Czarnikow v Roth, Schmidt & Co* (cited at 17.3.3) and other authorities).

### 17.3.6   *The* Davstone *and* Nikko *cases*

Does *Nikko v MEPC* (cited at 17.3.5) mean the parties can exclude the court from *all* aspects of a reference to an expert? An example of an expert clause which purported to do just that was considered in *Re Davstone Estates Ltd's leases, Manprop Ltd v O'Dell* [1969] 2 Ch 378. The leases said that the certificate of the lessors' expenses was to be final and 'not subject to challenge in any manner whatsoever'. The court held that this provision was void as contrary to public policy, as it ousted the jurisdiction of the courts on questions of law. The judge in *Nikko v MEPC* said that it was clear that it was not unlawful to exclude resort to the court in the circumstances of *Davstone* on the analogy of what Parliament had done to some kinds of arbitration with the 1979 Act: see 17.3.3. But it is Parliament which excluded the jurisdiction of the court from those specified kinds of arbitration, and exclusion of recourse from the decision of an expert is an act of the parties: and arguably the judge in *Nikko v MEPC* would reject as contrary to public policy an interpretation of a clause of the type found in the *Davstone* leases which prevented *any* recourse to the court on the grounds of fraud, partiality or mistake — even as narrowly as mistake is now defined.

### 17.3.7   The court will be excluded from most references

The practical effect of *Nikko v MEPC* (cited at 17.3.5) is that an implied term of a contract to refer a matter to an expert for determination does exclude the court from all aspects of a reference. This will be true except in those rare cases where it will be possible to say that the expert has asked himself the 'wrong question'. However, in the many cases where the right question is asked, but doubts persist as to whether the right answer is given, the expert's decision will not only be final but also 'judge-proof' and completely unchallengeable.

## 17.4   Other determinations by third parties

### 17.4.1   Arbitration

Can comparisons be made with other determinations by third parties, to see how the courts approach the question of the validity of decisions? Arbitration is the closest comparison. The public policy considerations are, apparently, the same for arbitrations as for expert references: *Re Davstone Estate Ltd's leases, Manprop Ltd v O'Dell* [1969] 2 Ch 378 at 386D.

### 17.4.2   Competitions

Sports and competitions provide interesting comparisons where the decision of a third party is relied on to settle an issue. The courts do not interfere with those who decide the winners of sport and other competitions: eg *Brown v Overbury* (1856) 11 Exch 715, *Sadler v Smith* (1869) 4 LR 214 and *Cipriani v Burnett* [1933] AC 83. The courts would not wish to adjudicate on who had won a competition unless there had been fraud.

### 17.4.3   Wagers

How far would the courts go in not interfering with decisions by agreed third parties? Would the court enforce a contract under which the parties agreed to abide by the toss of a coin? Many issues are settled that way every day, but probably not in circumstances where the law says that the parties intend to create legal relations. In any case, the court would not enforce such an arrangement on the grounds that the contract was by way of wager. The court has refused to enforce the decision of a valuer where the result of the valuation triggered consequences which seemed out of proportion, on the ground that the contract was by way of wager: see the strange story in *Rourke v Short* (1856) 5 El & Bl 904.

### 17.4.4   How did the expert reach his decision?

Comparisons with competition results are not inapt because the decision of an expert is often 'non-speaking', ie just the answer (or result) without any reasons or calculations. It is very difficult to find how an expert has reached a decision: it may actually have been by the toss of a coin. But that is the contract. If the parties have referred the matter to an expert for determination and agreed that reasons and calculations are unnecessary, they have to accept the risk that the decision may not have been arrived at by a professional investigation, because of the severe practical difficulties of proof. The parties would need evidence of the absence of a professional investigation before starting professional negligence proceedings against their expert, and mere suspicion that he had made his decision by tossing a coin would not be sufficient to found a challenge to the decision.

## 17.5   Conclusion

### 17.5.1   General dispute resolution more commonly referred to experts now

The crucial stage may soon be reached when the English courts will have to decide whether to dismiss a challenge to a decision by an expert on all disputes arising under a contract, both general and technical. References of this type are becoming more common. A clause referring all disputes under a construction contract to an expert has been upheld in the Australian courts: *Public Authorities Superannuation Board v Southern International Developments Corporation Pty Ltd* (1987) unreported: cited at 6.9.3.

### 17.5.2   A new form of dispute resolution?

The courts' reluctance to upset experts' decisions has recently become very much more marked. Will the courts apply different rules to decisions by experts on general, non-technical disputes? The extension of expert determination into general dispute resolution combined with this non-interventionist policy will produce a wider class of wrong and unchallengeable decisions. The law upholds experts' decisions because the parties have agreed to be bound, and not because of any special factor deriving from the status of the expert, the quality of the decision or the manner in which it was reached. Until recently, the technical nature of the question put to the expert was a special factor, but this is ceasing to be the case with the extension of expert determination into general dispute resolution. If the courts accept this development, a new form of dispute resolution will have been created, allowing parties' legal rights to be determined without the procedures and safeguards that have always been thought essential. This is a major public policy issue on which the courts may soon have to make a judgment.

# Precedents for an Accountancy Expert

## Important Note

These precedents are by way of example and will need careful adaptation for particular applications. They can also be used, suitably adapted, for references to experts other than accountants. See Bernstein and Reynolds for rent review precedents.

## I  Expert Clause

1 If the Vendors and the Purchasers are unable to agree on [the sales figure] by [date] the matter in dispute shall be referred, at the request of either the Vendors or the Purchasers, for decision to an independent Chartered Accountant (the 'Independent Accountant') who shall be appointed by agreement between the Vendors and the Purchasers, or, if they have not agreed within 14 days of the [first date above] [ date of request to refer by one of the parties], by the President for the time being of the Institute of Chartered Accountants in England and Wales ['the President'] on the application of either party. If an Independent Accountant has been appointed but is unable to complete the reference another Independent Accountant shall be appointed by the parties, or if they have not agreed on the appointment within 14 days of the request to do so by one of the parties, by the President.

[2 Optional provision for disclosing confidential documents or authorising disclosure from those in hands of third party.]

3 The Independent Accountant shall act as an expert and not as an arbitrator. The parties shall each have the right to make representations to the Independent Accountant. The decision of the Independent Accountant shall, in the absence of manifest error, be final and binding on the parties. All costs incurred by the Independent Accountant shall be borne by the Vendors and the Purchasers in equal shares unless the Independent Accountant determines otherwise. The amount (if any) which becomes payable by the Purchasers to the Vendors, or, as the case may be, repayable by the Vendors to the Purchasers, as a result of the Independent Accountant's decision shall become due and payable within seven days of publication of the decision. The Independent Accountant shall have the power to direct that interest on that amount, at the rate equal to [1 per cent — a compensatory rate] above the base rate of [clearing] bank, shall be paid by the Purchasers to the Vendors or repaid by the Vendors to the Purchasers as compensation for delay in receipt in respect of the period following the date on which the matter was referred to the Independent Accountant.

4 If the amount payable as a result of the Independent Accountant's decision is not paid by either the Vendors or the Purchasers within the period of seven days after publication of the Independent Accountant's decision, interest will accrue on that amount at the rate of [4 per cent — a penal rate] above the base rate of [clearing] bank.

# II  Appointment Letter

This form can be used where parties agree on the appointment of an expert without needing to apply to an appointing authority: in the other precedents it is assumed that the appointment is made by the President of the Institute of Chartered Accountants. Some appointing authorities have their own standard forms for application and appointment, and a fee is payable.

1 We refer to Clause [number] of the agreement between the Vendors and the Purchasers dated [date] by which the Purchasers acquired the whole of the issued share capital of XYZ plc from the Vendors ('the Agreement'): a copy of the agreement is enclosed.

2 Clause [number] of the Agreement provided that if the parties could not agree on [the sales figure], they should appoint an independent accountant to determine the figure. They have not been able to agree.

3 Accordingly the parties jointly* request you [Mr ABC] to determine [the sales figure].

4 Draft terms of reference are enclosed, which the parties have agreed: if you are prepared to accept the appointment, please indicate whether you also approve these draft terms.

* Or one party only: see 8.7.3. In these cases the letter should set out the part of the expert clause allowing one party only to appoint and the circumstances in which the other party has not joined in the application.

# III   Terms of Reference

1 We refer to the agreement [date] ('the Agreement') between [parties] by which the Vendors sold to the Purchasers the whole of the issued share capital of XYZ plc; the Purchasers' liability to make additional payments to the Vendors or, as the case may be, the Vendors' liability to make repayments to the Purchasers depends on whether, and, if so, by how much, XYZ plc's sales exceeded or fell short of the sum of £2 million in the year ended 31 December 1991.

2 Clause [number of expert clause] of the Agreement provided that if the parties had not agreed on [the sales figure] in clause [number] by [date] the matter was to be referred to an Independent Accountant acting as an expert and not as an arbitrator whose decision was to be final and binding and whose fees would be shared equally between the parties unless the Independent Accountant determined otherwise.

3 The parties disagree about the [sales figure]. As the parties were also unable to agree on who the Independent Accountant should be, they applied to the President of the Institute of Chartered Accountants requesting that he appoint an Independent Accountant.

4 The President of the Institute of Chartered Accountants appointed Mr ABC to be the Independent Accountant, by a letter [date].

5 The issue referred to Mr ABC is whether the [sales figure should include the sales of widgets by a subsidiary which are unconnected with the main business of XYZ plc].

6 The parties agree to pay Mr ABC's fees in equal shares and that his fees shall be charged at the rate of £xxx per hour plus reasonable expenses [or to pay Mr ABC's fees and expenses as Mr ABC directs].

[7 Mr ABC shall decide whether either the Vendors or the Purchasers are to pay or contribute to the costs incurred by the other party.]

[8 Provision to replace Mr ABC if he becomes incapacitated during the reference, if this is not contained in the expert clause.]

[9 Provision for the decision to include interest if not in the expert clause.]

[10 Optional provision for confidential and third party documents—if not in the expert clause.]

Signed by the expert and the parties.

# IV   Procedural Directions

1 Mr ABC will receive from the Vendors acting as agents for both the Vendors and the Purchasers [ here list the basic documents—the contract and other specified documents].

2 The Vendors* will send Mr ABC a letter setting out their case by [date—say 28 days from date of directions]. All documents relied on and/or referred to by the Vendors must be attached to that letter, unless they have already been supplied to Mr ABC under direction 1 above. The Vendors will send the Purchasers a copy of their letter and attachments at the same time as they are sent to Mr ABC.

3 The Purchasers* will send Mr ABC a letter setting out their case by [date—say 28 days from date of Vendors' letter]. All documents relied on and/or referred to by the Purchasers must be attached to the letter, unless they have already been supplied to Mr ABC under direction 1 or 2 above. The Purchasers will send the Vendors a copy of their letter and attachments at the same time as they are sent to Mr ABC.

[4 Optional provision for further submissions.]

5 Neither party has the right to call for a hearing at which witnesses would be examined. However, Mr ABC may meet the parties' accountants [and the parties themselves] either separately or together at his discretion.

6 Mr ABC may request either party or both parties to make further submissions, to be provided to Mr ABC and copied to the other party within [21] days of the request.

7 If Mr ABC decides he needs to take legal advice on the issue he is to determine, he shall instruct the [DEF] law firm after notifying the parties and obtaining their agreement to pay [DEF]'s fees.

[8 Arrangements to inspect a site or object—not usually necessary for accountancy experts.]

9 Either party has the right to apply to Mr ABC on two working days' notice given to Mr ABC and the other party.

10 Mr ABC shall issue a [non-]speaking decision within [10] weeks of the date of the latest submission.

11 All communications are to be sent to [list addresses for communications, with telephone and fax numbers]. All communications are to be sent by fax with a confirming copy sent by post.

Signed by the expert and the parties

Dated

* Note that in some cases orders are made for simultaneous submissions.

# V  Decision

1 I [ABC] was appointed to decide [define the issue: eg, whether the sales figure included the sales of widgets by the subsidiary etc] between the Vendors and the Purchasers under an agreement between the parties [dated].

2 [Here all the points in the terms of reference may be either recited, or the terms of reference themselves may be referred to by the following: The circumstances of the reference, the issue to be decided, my appointment and my fees were all provided for in Terms of Reference between the parties and myself [dated].]

3 Procedural directions for the reference were agreed on [date], and the parties made their submissions to me in accordance with those directions.

4 My decision is that the [sales of widgets by the subsidiary should be included in the sales figure]. [It will depend on the wording of the Agreement whether Mr ABC needs to go further and say what the sales figure is as a consequence, and how much interest the Purchasers should pay the Vendors following the lapse of time since the issue arose.]

[5 Reasons for the decision.]

[6 The Purchasers shall pay the Vendors' costs assessed at £xxx.]

7 My fees are £xxx and my expenses are £xx, payable [in equal shares by the Vendors and the Purchasers] or [payable by the Purchasers].

Signed          [ABC].

Dated...............

# Appendix B

# Appointment of Experts by the Law Society

**1 Law Society's guidelines on appointments and nominations of arbitrators and experts**

Reprinted from the *Law Society's Gazette*, 9 January 1991, 16.†

The Finance Committee has approved increased fees for presidential arbitration appointments (and nominations of independent experts) to take effect from 1 January 1991.

The level of fee will be determined by the amount in dispute, according to the table below.

Where there is no amount in dispute, the basic fee of £100 will apply.

The present flat-rate fee of £70 (plus VAT) was fixed in 1986. The new fee structure is intended to reflect inflation and generate additional income for the Society, part of which will be used to fund a new post for a lawyer to deal solely with processing these appointments.

| Amount in dispute | Fee (exclusive of VAT) |
|---|---|
| Below £10,000 | £100 |
| £10,001–£25,000 | £175 |
| £25,001–£50,000 | £250 |
| £50,001–£100,000 | £400 |
| £100,001–£250,000 | £500 |
| Above £250,000 | £1,000 |

**2 Arbitrators and Experts\* — Nominations and Appointments**

Reprinted from the *Law Society's Gazette*, 3 September 1986 , 2542.†

... So far as the Law Society is concerned, when such applications are received, solicitors are requested to supply the following:

1 a certified copy of the whole of the document containing the arbitration clause, showing the stamp duty (if liable) paid on the original;

160

2 an indication of the preferred profession, seniority and any special qualifications of the arbitrator;

3 the names of any members of that profession who are debarred from choice;

4 an estimate of the amount involved in the case;

5 an estimate of the amount of time any hearing will take;

6 the preferred location for any hearing;

7 the names, addresses, solicitors and references of all parties involved;

8 where proceedings have already been commenced in the courts, sufficient evidence, usually in the form of a sealed copy of an order under s 4 of the Arbitration Act 1950, that they have been stayed to enable the reference to arbitration to proceed;

9 a cheque in favour of the Law Society for [for new rates see above] to cover the recoupment fee and VAT for dealing with the appointment.

It is anticipated that these points will cover most of the usual cases. Should any other points arise, however, please contact the Law Society using reference GM Arb.

When a certified copy of the instrument creating the power to appoint or nominate has been obtained, it has to be perused to ensure that the President's power so to act has arisen and there follows a careful consideration of the discipline to which the arbitrator should belong, his seniority in his profession and any special knowledge and experience required of him in a particular case, based on the information supplied by the parties making the application.

This can involve careful liaison with the professional body to which the proposed arbitrator belongs, as it does in those cases where the head of another profession is required to appoint a solicitor, so that a suitable short-list of members of that profession from within the areas, both geographical and professional, that are required in the particular case, can be drawn up and from which the President may make his choice. Naturally, where the President is asked·to appoint a solicitor, similar considerations apply and in such circumstances, reference would, if necessary, be made to the local law society in the area concerned for its recommendations.

When an approved short-list has been prepared after all material considerations have been taken into account, it is placed before the President for him to indicate his order of choice. The possible arbitrators are subsequently contacted in that order until the first one is arrived at who is willing and able to take up the reference in the particular case. Thereafter, the formal appointment is prepared for signature by the President. It is then sent to the arbitrator with the certified copy of the instrument containing the arbitration clause and copies of the appointment are sent to the parties or to their representatives.

... It is for the solicitors who make the application to pay the fee on application, and it would then be a matter for them to raise with the other side or with the arbitrator, as appropriate, as to how the parties should contribute towards it ...

† *We are grateful to the Law Society's Gazette for permission to reproduce the above articles.*

* [Author's note] The only mention of experts appears in the heading, but many of the provisions will apply to experts as well as arbitrators. Those that apply to experts only with some modification are as follows: the references in guidelines 5 and 6 to a 'hearing' are not appropriate to every expert reference, and an order staying proceedings in guideline 8 would not be made under s4 of the Arbitration Act 1950.

# Rent Review Model Form — Variation C

**Determination** **in default of agreement to be either by arbitration or by independent valuer acting as expert (at the landlord's option) with alternative provisions for (a) upwards only review and (b) upwards or downwards review**

... yielding and paying to the landlord yearly rents ascertained in accordance with the next four clauses hereof without any deduction by equal quarterly payments in advance on the usual quarter days the first payment (being an apportioned sum) to be made on the date hereof

**Clause 1**

Definitions

In this lease 'review date' means the     day of in the year 19    and in every    year thereafter and 'review period' means the period starting with any review date up to the next review date or starting with the last review date up to the end of the term hereof

**Clause 2**

The yearly rent shall be:

(A) until the first review date the rent of £    and

Provisions for revision of rent in upwards only review

*(B) during each successive review period a rent equal to the rent previously payable hereunder or such revised rent as may be ascertained as herein provided whichever be the greater*

OR

For revision of rent in upwards or downwards review

*(B)(i) during each successive review period such revised rent as may be ascertained as herein provided and*

*(B)(ii) in the event of a revised rent not being ascertained as herein provided the rent payable for the relevant review period shall be the rent payable immediately prior to the commencement of such period*

**Clause 3**
Ascertainment
of amount by
arbitrator or by
independent
valuer at the
landlord's
option

Such revised rent for any review period may be agreed at any time between the landlord and the tenant or (in the absence of agreement) determined not earlier than the relevant review date at the option of the landlord either by an arbitrator or by an independent valuer (acting as an expert and not as an arbitrator) such arbitrator or valuer to be nominated in the absence of agreement by or on behalf of the President for the time being of the Royal Institution of Chartered Surveyors on the application of the landlord (in exercise of the said option) made not earlier than six months before the relevant review date *but not later than the end of the relevant review period* and so that in the case of such arbitration or valuation the revised rent to be awarded or determined by the arbitrator or valuer shall be such as he shall decide is the yearly rent at which the demised premises might reasonably be expected to be let at the relevant review date

(A) On the following assumptions at that date:

(i) That the demised premises:

(a) are available to let on the open market without a fine or premium with vacant possession by a willing landlord to a willing tenant for a term of [10] years or the residue then unexpired of the term of this lease (whichever be the longer)

(b) are to be let as a whole subject to the terms of this lease (other than the amount of the rent hereby reserved but including the provisions for review of that rent)

(c) are fit and available for immediate occupation

(d) may be used for any of the purposes permitted by this lease as varied or extended by any licence granted pursuant thereto

(ii) That the covenants herein contained on the part of *the landlord and* the tenant have been fully performed and observed

(iii) That no work has been carried out to the demised premises which has diminished the rental value and that in case the demised premises have been destroyed or damaged they have been fully restored

(iv) That no reduction is to be made to take account of any rental concession which on a new letting with vacant possession might be granted to the incoming tenant for a period within which its fitting out works would take place.

(B) But disregarding:

(i) any effect on rent of the fact that the tenant its sub-tenants or their respective predecessors in title have been in occupation of the demised premises

(ii) any goodwill attached to the demised premises by reason of the carrying on thereat of the business of the tenant its sub-tenants or their predecessors in title in their respective businesses and

(iii) any increase in rental value of the demised premises attributable to the existence at the relevant review date of any improvement to the demised premises or any part thereof carried out with consent where required otherwise than in pursuance of an obligation to the landlord or its predecessors in title except obligations requiring compliance with statutes or directions of Local Authorities or other bodies exercising powers under statute or Royal Charter either (a) by the tenant its sub-tenants or their respective predecessors in title during the said term or during any period of occupation prior thereto arising out of an agreement to grant such term or *(b) by any tenant or sub-tenant of the demised premises before the commencement of the term hereby granted so long as the landlord or its predecessors in title have not since the improvement was carried out had vacant possession of the relevant part of the demised premises*

**Clause 4**

IT IS HEREBY FURTHER PROVIDED in relation to the ascertainment and payment of revised rent as follows:

Further
provisions as to
arbitration

(A) (In the case of arbitration) the arbitration shall be conducted in accordance with the Arbitration Acts 1950 and 1979 or any statutory modification or re-enactment thereof for the time being in force with the further provision that if the arbitrator nominated pursuant to Clause 3 hereof shall die or decline to act the President for the time being of the Royal Institution of

Chartered Surveyors or the person acting on his behalf he may on the application of either the landlord or the tenant by writing discharge the arbitrator and appoint another in his place

As to independent valuation

(B) (In the case of determination by a valuer)
(i) the fees and expenses of the valuer including the cost of his nomination shall be borne equally by the landlord and the tenant who shall otherwise each bear their own costs and

(ii) the valuer shall afford the landlord and the tenant an opportunity to make representations to him and

(iii) if the valuer nominated pursuant to Clause 3 hereof shall die delay or become unwilling, unfit or incapable of acting or if for any other reason the President for the time being of the Royal Institution of Chartered Surveyors or the person acting on his behalf shall in his absolute discretion think fit he may on the application of either the landlord or the tenant by writing discharge the valuer and appoint another in his place

As to memoranda of ascertainment

(C) When the amount of any rent to be ascertained as hereinbefore provided shall have been so ascertained memoranda thereof shall thereupon be signed by or on behalf of the landlord and the tenant and annexed to this lease and the counterpart thereof and the landlord and the tenant shall bear their own costs in respect thereof

As to interim payments and final adjustments upwards only review

*(D)(i) If the revised rent payable on and from any review date has not been agreed by that review date rent shall continue to be payable at the rate previously payable and forthwith upon the revised rent being ascertained, the tenant shall pay to the landlord any shortfall between the rent and the revised rent payable up to and on the preceding quarter day together with interest on any shortfall at the seven day deposit rate of BANK such interest to be calculated on a day-to-day basis from the relevant review date on which it would have been payable if the revised rent had then been ascertained to the date of actual payment of any shortfall and the interest so payable shall be recoverable in the same manner as rent in arrear*

OR

upwards or
downwards
review

*(D)(i)  If the revised rent payable on and from any review date has not been agreed by that review date rent shall continue to be payable at the rate previously payable and forthwith upon the revised rent being ascertained the tenant shall pay to the landlord any shortfall between the rent and the revised rent or as the case may be the landlord shall pay to the tenant any excess of the rent paid over the revised rent payable up to and on the preceding quarter day together with interest on any shortfall or as the case may be any excess at the seven day deposit rate of        BANK such interest to be calculated on a day-to-day basis from the relevant review date on which it would have been payable if the revised rent had then been ascertained to the date of actual payment of any shortfall or any excess and the interest so payable shall be recoverable in the same manner as rent in arrear or as the case may be as a debt*

(ii) for the purposes of this proviso the revised rent shall be deemed to have been ascertained on the date when the same has been agreed between the landord and the tenant or as the case may be the date of the award of the arbitrator or of the determination by the valuer

(E) If either the landlord or the tenant shall fail to pay any costs awarded against it in the case of an arbitration or the moiety of the fees and expenses of the valuer under the provisions hereof within twenty-one days of the same being demanded by the arbitrator or the valuer (as the case may be) the other shall be entitled to pay the same and the amount so paid shall be repaid by the party chargeable on demand.

As to notice by
the tenant to
trigger
landlord's
application

*(F) Whenever a revised rent in respect of any review period has not been agreed between the landlord and the tenant before the relevant review date and where no agreement has been reached as to the appointment of an arbitrator or valuer nor has the landlord made any application to the President for the time being of the Royal Institution of Chartered Surveyors as hereinbefore provided the tenant may serve on the landlord notice in writing referring to this provision and containing a proposal as to the amount of such revised rent (which shall not be less than the rent payable immediately before the commencement of the relevant review period) and the amount so proposed shall be deemed to*

*have been agreed by the landlord and the tenant as the revised rent for the relevant review period and sub-clause (D)(i) hereof shall apply accordingly unless the landlord shall make such application as aforesaid within three months after service of such notice by the tenant. Time shall be of the essence in respect of this provision.*

*Reproduced with the kind permission of The Royal Institution of Chartered Surveyors.*

# Appendix D

# Precedent for Share Valuation

1 The expression 'Fair Price' means the price which the auditors of the Company state in writing to be in their opinion the fair value of the shares on a sale between a willing seller and a willing purchaser (taking no account of whether the shares do or do not carry control of the Company) and, if the Company is then carrying on business as a going concern, on the assumption that it will continue to do so. The Fair Price shall be assessed at the date of service of the Transfer Notice and by reference to the information available to the company at that date.

2 In stating the Fair Price the auditors (whose charges shall be borne by the Company) shall be considered to be acting as experts and not as arbitrators and their decision shall be final and binding on the parties.

# Appendix E

# Precedent for Assessing Trustee's Remuneration in Capital Market Trust Deeds

In the event of the Trustee and the Issuer failing to agree:
(1) upon the amount of the remuneration; or
(2) upon whether their duties shall be of an exceptional nature or otherwise outside the scope of the normal duties of the Trustee under these presents, or upon such additional remuneration,
such matters shall be determined by a merchant bank (acting as an expert and not as an arbitrator) selected by the Trustee and approved by the Issuer, or, failing such approval, nominated (on the application of the Trustee) by the President for the time being of the Law Society of England and Wales (the expenses involved in such nomination and the fees of such merchant bank being payable by the Issuer) and the determination of any such merchant bank shall be final and binding upon the Trustee and the Issuer.

# Appendix F

# List of Appointing Authorities

The Association of Consulting Engineers
Alliance House
12 Caxton Street
London
SW1H 0QL
071–222 6557


The Chartered Institute of Arbitrators
24 Angel Gate
London
EC1V 2RS
071–837 4483


The Chartered Institute of Management Accountants
63 Portland Place
London
W1N 4AB
071–637 2311


The Chartered Institute of Patent Agents
Staple Inn Buildings
High Holborn
London
WC1V 7PZ
071–405 9450


The Incorporated Society of Valuers and Auctioneers
3 Cadogan Gate
London
SW1X 0AS
071–235 2282

The Institute of Actuaries
Staple Inn Hall
High Holborn
London
WC1V 7QJ
071–242 0106

The Institute of Chartered Accountants in England and Wales
Moorgate Place
London
EC2P 2BJ
071–628 7060

The Institute of Petroleum
61 New Cavendish Street
London
W1M 8AR
071–636 1004

The Law Society
113 Chancery Lane
London
WC2A 1PL
071–242 1222

Royal Institute of British Architects
66 Portland Place
London
W1N 4AD
071–580 5533

The Royal Institution of Chartered Surveyors
12 Great George Street
London
SW1P 3AE
071–222 7000

# Appendix G

# RICS Application Form

**Form AS2 (July 1991)**

THE ROYAL INSTITUTION
OF CHARTERED SURVEYORS
Arbitration Service

### APPLICATION FOR THE APPOINTMENT / NOMINATION OF AN ARBITRATOR / INDEPENDENT EXPERT BY THE PRESIDENT OF THE ROYAL INSTITUTION OF CHARTERED SURVEYORS

**(Other than commercial property rent review and Agricultural Holdings Act cases)**

All details must be typewritten

| | |
|---|---|
| I / We | hereby request the President of the |
| Royal Institution of Chartered Surveyors to [ appoint / nominate ] an [ Arbitrator / Independent Expert ] | |
| *(delete as appropriate)* to act in the case described overleaf | |
| **OR** | |
| The application for the appointment / nomination of an Arbitrator / Independent Expert to which the following details refer was made in a letter from: | |
| dated: | ref: |
| **Applicant / Claimant**<br>(full names and address) | |
| **Applicant's Solicitors**<br>(name, address, telephone number<br>and reference) | |
| **Applicant's Surveyors**<br>(name, address, telephone number<br>and reference) | |
| **Other Party / Respondent**<br>(full names and address)<br>and reference) | |
| **Other Party's Solicitors**<br>(name, address, telephone number<br>and reference) | |
| **Other Party's Surveyors**<br>(name, address, telephone number<br>and reference) | |
| **To which of the above should communications on this matter be addressed**<br>(name of individual if known)? | |

**Conflicts of Interest**

If you think that there are any Chartered Surveyors who should not be considered for appointment / nomination because they do not fulfil the criteria referred to in the attached policy statement, please state their names here, together with full reasons supporting your views (continue on a separate sheet if necessary). It is emphasised that, while the President will give careful consideration to any representations, he will reach his own decision as to who shall be appointed / nominated.

**Nature of Dispute**

(including approximate sum of money in dispute and address of premises, if relevant; continue on a separate sheet if necessary)

**Agreement to Refer**

Which clause of the contract or other relevant agreement provides for the dispute to be referred to the decision of a surveyor appointed / nominated by the President of the Royal Institution of Chartered Surveyors? A copy of the signed contract or comparable document should accompany this application. If this does not incorporate provision for the settlement of disputes by an arbitrator / independent expert appointed / nominated by the President then a separate agreement making such provision, signed by both parties will be required before any appointment / nomination can be made, except in cases where the appointment/ nomination is made by order of the Court.

We accept that in some circumstances the appointment will be made by the President through one of his Vice-Presidents or duly appointed agents and this is the basis upon which the application is submitted to you and upon which the application will be entertained. We accept that in special circumstances (to be decided by the President) it may be inappropriate for the President to effect the appointment and in these circumstances the appointment may be effected by a Vice President in his own name.

**Fees**

Except in cases where the President is designated by statute as the appointing authority or the appointment is to be made by Order of the Court a fee of £117.50 (ie £100.00 plus VAT), non-returnable must accompany all applications for appointments by the President.

**We enclose** a cheque for £117.50 / copy of the Court Order directing that this appointment be made and we undertake to be responsible for payment of the professional fees and costs of the Surveyor appointed, including any fees and costs due where a negotiated settlement is reached before the award or determination being taken up.

Signed ..............................................................

Dated ........................................................    ..............................................................

To be returned to : The Arbitrations Section, RICS, Surveyor Court,
Westwood Way, Coventry, CV4 8JE
Tel: 071 222 7000 (or Local Calls: 0203 694757) Fax: 071 334 3802

*Reproduced by kind permission of the Royal Institution of Chartered Surveyors.*

# Appendix H

# ISVA Application Form

**Appointment of an Arbitrator\* Surveyor\* Valuer\***

We refer to the lease of premises known as              dated        and made between              the lessor(s) of the First Part              the lessee(s) of the Second Part and        of the Third Part*
wherein provision is made for the President of this Society (or for the President of the Incorporated Society of Auctioneers and Landed Property Agents, which Society merged in 1968 to form the ISVA) to appoint an Arbitrator*/Surveyor*/Valuer* and we hereby request that such an appointment now be made for the purpose of determining the following matters in dispute between us

We agree jointly and severally to take up within seven days of its publication the Award of the Arbitrator (Surveyor or Valuer) whose decision shall be final and binding and in any event to pay his/her fees and expenses in connection with the Award as he/she may determine.

1 Signed (for the lessor(s))
  Capacity (eg Agents)
  Address


  Dated

2 Signed (for the lessee(s))
  Capacity (eg Agents)
  Address


  Dated

3 Signed (for the Third Party)
Capacity (eg Agents)
Address


Dated

Pursuant to the request made by the parties hereto, I [name], as President of the Incorporated Society of Valuers and Auctioneers hereby appoint          of          as    Arbitrator*/Surveyor*/Valuer* to determine this dispute.
Signed
Dated this      day of      19

I hereby accept the appointment of Arbitrator*/Surveyor*/Valuer* in the above matter.
Signed
Dated this      day of      19


* Delete as required

When completed, this form should be returned to the Incorporated Society of Valuers and Auctioneers, 3 Cadogan Gate, London, SW1X 0AS, marked for the attention of the Professional Services Officer.

*Reproduced by kind permission of the Incorporated Society of Valuers and Auctioneers.*

# Glossary

Every subject grows its own jargon and borrows jargon from its neighbours. Here is a list, with a brief explanation, of some of the technical expressions used in this book or appearing in other textbooks or in the law reports.

**Ad hoc reference**  A **reference** arranged after a dispute has arisen: see 8.2.4. It can have this meaning in **arbitration** law, but can also mean a *supervised* **arbitration**: see 10.2.3. There are no instances of a supervised reference to an **expert**.

**Appointing authority**  A body specified by the parties to appoint an **expert** (or an **arbitrator**) if they cannot agree on one: see 10.2.3.

**Appointment**  An act by which the parties or an **appointing authority** establish the identity of the **expert** to conduct the **reference**. Contrast **nomination**.

**Appraisal** or **appraisement**  The act of valuation.

**Appraiser**  Valuer.

**Arbitration**  A form of private dispute resolution between the two parties to a contract, subject to the law of **arbitration**: an unavoidably circular definition: see Mustill and Boyd, pp 38–50. For a full account of the differences between **arbitration** and **expert determination**, see Chapter 15.

**Arbitrator**  An individual charged with resolving a dispute submitted to **arbitration**.

**Award**   The judgment issued by an **arbitrator**. This expression is sometimes used for **experts' decisions** as well.

**Certificate**   The form of **decision** issued by certain **experts**, such as accountants: not to be confused with certificates issued under a construction contract (see 7.4) or a share certificate.

**Conflicted out**   Prevented from accepting an **appointment as expert** by conflicts of interest: 10.8.3.

**Construction**   Means either (i) interpretation: or (ii) building/engineering.

**Decision**   What an **expert** issues as the result of his work, otherwise known as an **award, certificate** or **determination**.

**Determination**   See **Decision**: also a descriptive label for the subject, derived from the decision-making process.

**Disputes clause**   The clause in a contract which says how disputes are to be handled: eg by **reference** to an **expert, arbitration** or litigation.

**Expert**   Someone appointed by parties to a contract to decide an issue in accordance with the terms of that contract and in a manner not subject to the law of **arbitration**; for the differences from being an **arbitrator**, see Chapter 15.

**Expert clause**   The expression used in this book for the clause containing the machinery for referring questions to an **expert** for **decision**: see Chapter 8.

**Expert determination**   The process by which an **expert** decides questions referred to him.

**Formulated dispute**   An issue on which the parties have taken defined positions: see 15.5.

**Impeach, impugn**   These words mean the challenge of **experts' decisions** by parties and the court declaring **decisions** invalid.

**Indicia** The plural of **indicium**.

**Indicium** A Latin word meaning a sign, but translated 'guide-line' in this book: see 15.4.

**Miscarriage** Serious breach of contract: see 13.4.

**Nomination** The act by which a party proposes an **expert** (or an **arbitrator**) for **appointment**.

**Non-speaking valuation** or **decision** A **decision** unaccompanied by reasons or calculations: see 13.7.

**Official Referee** A judge dealing mainly with building/engineering cases.

**Quasi-arbitrator** Status of **expert** giving him immunity from suit, now obsolete: see 14.6.

**Referee** The person to whom an issue is referred, in whatever capacity. Not to be confused with **Official Referee**.

**Reference** The procedure under which an **expert** (or an **arbitrator**) decides issues.

**Speaking valuation** or **decision** A **decision** which provides reasons and/or calculations: see 13.7.

**Terms of reference** Terms agreed between the parties and usually the **expert** as well about the matters to be decided by the **expert** and his **appointment**: see 11.4. The expression is also used in a similar way in **arbitration**.

**Umpirage** The process by which an **umpire** decides between the views of two party-appointed **experts**. An obsolete expression: for an example, see 14.3.2.

**Umpire** A third **expert**, usually appointed by two party-appointed **experts**: see 9.8. In **arbitrations** it is not uncommon for the **umpire** to be known as the 'third **arbitrator**' or the 'president', and for him to be appointed by the **appointing authority** supervising the **arbitration**.

# Further reading

## Books

Ronald Bernstein, *Handbook of Arbitration Practice*, Sweet & Maxwell in conjunction with the Chartered Institute of Arbitrators, London, 1987.

Ronald Bernstein and Kirk Reynolds, *Handbook of Rent Review*, Sweet & Maxwell, London, 1981: looseleaf and continuously updated.

Matthieu de Boisseson, *Le Droit francais de l'arbitrage*, GLN Joly, Paris, 1990.

*Chitty on Contracts*, 26th edn, Sweet & Maxwell, London, 1989.

Nigel Eastaway and Harry Booth, *Practical Share Valuation*, Butterworths, London, 1983.

Ed: Karl J Mackie, *A Handbook of Dispute Resolution: ADR in Action*, Routledge and Sweet & Maxwell, London and New York, 1991.

Sir Anthony May, *Keating on Building Contracts*, 5th edn, Sweet & Maxwell, London, 1991.

Sir Michael Mustill and Stewart Boyd, *Commercial Arbitration*, 2nd edn, Butterworths, London, 1989.

Ed: Glyn Saunders, *Tolley's Tax Planning 1991*, volume 2, Tolley Publishing Company limited.

Anthony Walton and Mary Vitoria, *Russell on Arbitration*, 20th edn, Stevens & Sons, London, 1982.

## Articles

Michael Buhler, 'Technical Expertise: An Additional Means for Preventing or Settling Commercial Disputes', *Journal of International Arbitration*, March 1989, pp 135–157.

Terence Burke and Christine Chinkin, 'Expert determination as a viable alternative to arbitration and litigation', [1989] *International Construction Law Review*, p 40.

Terence Burke and Christine Chinkin, 'Drafting alternative dispute resolution clauses', [1990] *International Construction Law Review*, p 444.

Lawrence Collins and Dorothy Livingston, 'Aspects of Conclusive Evidence Clauses', [1974] *Journal of Business Law*, p 212.

Jonathan Gaunt QC, 'What makes an award judge-proof?', [1991] *Estates Gazette* 28, p 70.

Paul A Jaffe, 'Judicial Supervision of Commercial Arbitration in England', (1989) *Arbitration* vol 55, p 184.

John Kendall and Steven Dark, 'Countering Confidentiality Agreements', (1991) *Law Society's Gazette* vol 31, p 14.

Mark C McGaw, 'Adjudicators, Experts, and keeping out of Court', *Current Developments in Construction Law*, fifth annual construction conference organised by the Centre of Construction Law and Management, King's College, London, 1991.

# Index